Studies On

Daniel

and

Revelation

A Compilation

By
Kraid Ashbaugh

TEACH Services, Inc.
New York

2005   06   07   08   09   10   11   12   ·   5   4   3   2   1

Copyright © 1988, 2004 TEACH Services, Inc.
ISBN-10: 1-57258-284-7
ISBN-13: 978-1-57258-284-2
Library of Congress Control Number: 2004106599

Published by

TEACH Services, Inc.
www.TEACHServices.com

CONTENTS

The Reason for Printing this Book v

Key to Abbreviations of E.G. White Book Titles vi

Encouragement for the Study of Daniel viii

Outline of Daniel x

Daniel 1 1

Daniel 2 5

Daniel 3 13

Daniel 4 19

Daniel 5 25

Daniel 6 30

Daniel 7 36

Daniel 8 43

Daniel 9 48

Daniel 10 54

Daniel 11 57

Daniel 12 72

Encouragement for the Study of Revelation 77

Outline of Revelation 78

Revelation 1 83

Revelation 2 88

Revelation 3 93

Revelation 4 99

Revelation 5 102

Revelation 6 105

STUDIES ON DANIEL AND REVELATION

Revelation 7. 110

Revelation 8. 114

Revelation 9. 121

Revelation 10 127

Revelation 11 130

Revelation 12 136

Revelation 13 143

Revelation 14 151

Revelation 15 158

Revelation 16 160

Revelation 17 166

Revelation 18 171

Revelation 19 176

Revelation 20 180

Revelation 21 184

Revelation 22 188

THE REASON FOR PRINTING THIS BOOK

The books of Daniel and the Revelation should be bound together and published—showing that they are related to the same subjects. See TM117 for full text.

The prophecies of Daniel and the Revelation should be printed in small books with necessary explanations added. See full text in 8T160.

This little book is printed especially for Bible students. Explanations have been kept to a minimum. Ellen White clarifications have not been quoted verbatim, but only the thought has been suggested. The reader is urged to look up the actual reference.

KEY TO ABBREVIATIONS OF
E. G. WHITE BOOK TITLES

Key/Book Title

AA–The Acts of the Apostles

AH–The Adventist Home

BC–The Seventh-day Adventist Bible Commentary, Volumes 1–7

CD–Counsels on Diet and Foods

CG–Child Guidance

CH–Counsels on Health

ChS–Christian Service

CM–Colporteur Ministry

COL–Christ's Object Lessons

CS–Counsels on Stewardship

CSW–Counsels on Sabbath School Work

CT–Counsels to Teachers, Parents, and Students

CW–Counsels to Writers and Editors

DA–Desire of Ages

Ed–Education

Ev–Evangelism

EW–Early Writings

FILB–Faith I Live By

FE–Fundamentals of Christian Education

GC–The Great Controversy

GW–Gospel Workers

KEY TO ABBREVIATIONS OF
E. G. WHITE BOOK TITLES

HP–In Heavenly Places

LS–Life Sketches

MB–Thoughts from the Mount of Blessing

MH–The Ministry of Healing

ML–My Life Today

MM–Medical Ministry

MS–Manuscript (unpublished document)

MYP–Messages to Young People

OHC–Our High Calling

PK–Prophets and Kings

PP–Patriarchs and Prophets

RH–The Review and Herald (magazine)

SC–Steps to Christ

SD–Sons and Daughters of God

SG–Spiritual Gifts, Volumes 1–4

SDABD–Seventh-day Adventist Bible Dictionary

SL–The Sanctified Life

SM–Selected Messages, Books 1–3

SP–Spirit of Prophecy, Volumes 1–4

ST–Signs of the Times (magazine)

SR–The Story of Redemption

T–Testimonies for the Church, Volumes 1–9

Te–Temperance

TM–Testimonies to Ministers

WM–Welfare Ministry

ENCOURAGEMENT FOR THE STUDY OF DANIEL

Daniel's prophecies should be carefully studied just now as they apply to our very time, the last days of this earth's history, PK547.

Daniel's messages, God-given, are in a special sense for these very times, TM113, 4BC1166.

A better understanding of Daniel and the Revelation will lead to a better spiritual life, TM114.

Daniel and the Revelation require special study, and every consecrated teacher should endeavor to study and present in the clearest way the Revelation of Jesus that He personally gave to John, Ed191.

The more loyal we are to the third angel's message, the better we'll understand Daniel, of which the Revelation is the supplement, 2SM114.

Those studying Christ's life sincerely will find in Daniel and the Revelation Spirit-filled truth, activating irrepressible forces, FE473.

Both Daniel and the Revelation give vital directions to men from God in regard to occurrences that will transpire when the history of this world will be coming to an end, GC741.

Teachers should increasingly treasure God's instruction that is so clearly given in the books of Daniel and the Revelation, 6T131.

Jesus highly recommended to His disciples the study of Daniel's prophecy when He said, "Whoso readeth let him understand," DA234.

Daniel and the Revelation explain each other, and they are to be understood as witnesses in the world, 7BC949.

Daniel is a prophecy, a book that was sealed; Revelation is a revealing, a book unsealed; so they are one, 7BC971.

A much more careful study of Daniel and the Revelation is needed now than ever before, CW65.

Because time is running out, and we are faced with the dangers of the events of the end of time, we are admonished to pray, study, be alert, and put into practice the instruction given in Daniel and the Revelation, 6T128.

OUTLINE OF DANIEL

Chapter 1–Earthly authorities are shown that a vegetarian diet without alcohol promotes physical and mental strength and health.

Chapter 2–The restoration of the territory of the Theocracy. The metal man.

Chapter 3–Earthly authorities must not enforce worship. The fiery furnace.

Chapter 4–Earthly authorities must be humble, not taking credit that belongs to God. Nebuchadnezzar's insanity.

Chapter 5–Earthly authorities must not use alcohol nor blaspheme God. Belshazzar's feast.

Chapter 6–Earthly authorities must not forbid worship. Daniel in the lions' den.

Chapter 7–The restoration of the King of the Theocracy. The four beasts.

Chapter 8, 9–The restoration of the sanctuary of the Theocracy. The ram and the goat.

Chapter 10, 11, 12–The restoration of the citizens of the Theocracy. Details from the closing years of Persia to the New Earth prophesied.

Book of DANIEL

DANIEL 1

1. In the third year of the reign of Jehoiakim king of Judah came Nebuchadnezzar king of Babylon unto Jerusalem, and besieged it.

2. And the Lord gave Jehoiakim king of Judah into his hand, with part of the vessels of the house of God: which he carried into the land of Shinar to the house of his god; and he brought the vessels into the treasure house of his god.

3. ¶ And the king spake unto Ashpenaz the master of his eunuchs, that he should bring certain of the children of Israel, and the king's secd, and of the princes;

"The king's seed." The four youth were of the royal line, FE77, Ed54, MH148. Daniel was eighteen, 4T570.

4. Children in whom was no blemish, but well favoured, and skilful in all wisdom, and cunning in knowledge, and understanding science, and such as had ability in them to stand in the king's palace, and whom they might teach the learning and the tongue of the Chaldeans.

"The Chaldeans. A designation for scholars, sorcerers, astrologers, and magicians. Since in the Neo-Babylonian Empire the Chaldeans occupied all high offices, including the priesthood, the ethnic name seems to have become a designation for the priestly work and office, which included the arts of divination" SDABD.

5. And the king appointed them a daily provision of the king's meat, and of the wine which he drank: so nourishing them three years, that at the end thereof they might stand before the king.

6. Now among these were of the children of Judah, Daniel, Hananiah, Mishael, and Azariah:

7. Unto whom the prince of the eunuchs gave names: for he gave unto Daniel the name of Belteshazzar; and to Hananiah, of Shadrach; and to Mishael, of Meshach, and to Azariah, of Abednego.

8. ¶ But Daniel purposed in his heart that he would not defile himself with the portion of the king's meat, nor with the wine which he drank: therefore he requested of the prince of the eunuchs that he might not defile himself.

"But Daniel." Many young men today will also witness for God in legislatures, courts, and palaces, Ed262. Like Enoch, they walked with God, MM276. To glorify God was the most powerful motive with Daniel, 4BC1170. Daniel illustrates a sanctified character, FE80. Daniel was the leader of the group, and had he failed, the others would also have given up, MS113, 1901. These youth were designated by God to bring the heathen a knowledge of Him, and as they honored God, He honored them, 6T219. It was their fidelity to the Scriptures that kept them faithful, PK428.

9. Now God had brought Daniel into favour and tender love with the prince of the eunuchs.

10. And the prince of the eunuchs said unto Daniel, I fear my lord the king, who hath appointed your meat and your drink: for why should he see your faces worse liking than the children which are of your sort? then shall ye make me endanger my head to the king.

11. Then said Daniel to Melzar, whom the prince of the eunuchs had set over Daniel, Hananiah, Mishael, and Azariah,

12. Prove thy servants, I beseech thee, ten days; and let them give us pulse to eat, and water to drink.

"Give us pulse." ("vegetables" RSV, NEB) This first chapter is the strongest argument on temperance that could be given, MS13, 1901. They had not eaten flesh meat before, 4BC1166, 1167. Cancer and disease is largely caused by meat eating,

9T159. Flesh food is harmful because of its stimulating effect and disease increase in animals, Ed203. Daniel 1 makes void the argument that one needs meat or a large variety of food, MS 73, 1896.

13. Then let our countenances be looked upon before thee, and the countenance of the children that eat of the portion of the king's meat: and as thou seest, deal with thy servants.

14. So he consented to them in this matter, and proved them ten days.

15. And at the end of ten days their countenances appeared fairer and fatter in flesh than all the children which did eat the portion of the king's meat.

16. Thus Melzar took away the portion of their meat, and the wine that they should drink; and gave them pulse.

"Thus Melzar took away." Christian perfection is not possible if one indulges appetite, 2T400, but victory here means victory on every other point, HP194, so remember that a victory over appetite is available through Christ, 9T156. Health reform is defined as a selection of the most healthful food prepared in the most healthful manner, ML32. True temperance dispenses with everything harmful and uses healthful things sensibly, Te132, PP562. Self-denial is an evidence to non-professors that those practicing self-denial are true Christians, 9T70.

17. ¶ As for these four children, God gave them knowledge and skill in all learning and wisdom: and Daniel had understanding in all visions and dreams.

"God gave them." Teachers may have help from God as Daniel did, CT456. They did not feel that God's blessing was a substitute for the best effort on their part, 4BC1167. Daniel's history, as well as Joseph's, shows what God can do when there is a wholehearted yielding to God, Ed56. As Daniel demonstrated, the intellectual powers increase in direct proportion to the increase of the spiritual powers, ML47. Self-control is the greatest triumph Christ gives to us, 4T235. To study the Bible

efficiently, the mind must be kept clear by a careful diet, TM114. Both physical and moral health are affected by the diet, FE143.

18. Now at the end of the days that the king had said he should bring them in, then the prince of the eunuchs brought them in before Nebuchadnezzar.

19. And the king communed with them; and among them all was found none like Daniel, Hananiah, Mishael, and Azariah: therefore stood they before the king.

20. And in all matters of wisdom and understanding, that the king inquired of them, he found them ten times better than all the magicians and astrologers that were in all his realm.

Magicians: Those who, as professionals or amateurs, practiced magic. Such people are mentioned in the Bible under different names, such as sorcerers, witches, soothsayers. Magicians were found in great numbers in Egypt (Gen. 41:8; Ex. 7:11) and Mesopotamia (Dan. 1:20; 2:2). SDABD.

"Astrologers." Hebrew "ashshaphim," Aramaic "ashephin" (Dan. 1:20; 2:2,10,27; 4:7; 5:7,11,15), practitioners of magic arts. But the particular branch or branches of magic in which these men engaged is not known. The RSV always renders the Hebrew and Aramaic terms "enchanters," SDABD.

21. And Daniel continued even unto the first year of king Cyrus.

DANIEL 2

1. And in the second year of the reign of Nebuchadnezzar, Nebuchadnezzar dreamed dreams, wherewith his spirit was troubled, and his sleep brake from him.

2. Then the king commanded to call the magicians, and the astrologers, and the sorcerers, and the Chaldeans, for to shew the king his dreams. So they came and stood before the king.

"Sorcerers." One who practices witchcraft or employs powers gained from the assistance and control of evil spirits, though in some instances certain terms thus translated may refer to one possessing a knowledge of chemistry and physics that enable him to give demonstrations that the ignorant would regard as supernatural feats, SDABD. "Chaldeans" See 1:4.

3. And the king said unto them, I have dreamed a dream, and my spirit was troubled to know the dream.

4. Then spake the Chaldeans to the king in Syriack, O king, live for ever: tell thy servants the dream, and we will shew the interpretation.

"Tell thy servants the dream." Nebuchadnezzar, suspicious and dissatisfied with their evasiveness, commanded them with threat of death and promise of wealth and honor to tell him the dream itself, PK492.

5. The king answered and said to the Chaldeans, The thing is gone from me: if ye will not make known unto me the dream, with the interpretation thereof, ye shall be cut in pieces, and your houses shall be made a dunghill.

6. But if ye shew the dream, and the interpretation thereof, ye shall receive of me gifts and rewards and great honour: therefore shew me the dream, and the interpretation thereof.

7. They answered again and said, Let the king tell his servants the dream, and we will shew the interpretation of it.

8. The king answered and said, I know of certainty that ye would gain the time, because ye see the thing is gone from me.

"The king answered." "It is clear to me that you are trying to gain time because you see that my intention has been declared." NEB.

9. But if ye will not make known unto me the dream, there is but one decree for you: for ye have prepared lying and corrupt words to speak before me, till the time be changed: therefore tell me the dream, and I shall know that ye can shew me the interpretation thereof.

10. ¶ The Chaldeans answered before the king, and said, There is not a man upon the earth that can shew the king's matter: therefore there is no king, lord, nor ruler, that asked such things at any magician, or astrologer, or Chaldean.

11. And it is a rare thing that the king requireth, and there is none other that can shew it before the king, except the gods, whose dwelling is not with flesh.

"The gods, whose dwelling is not with flesh." An untrue heathen concept: "This is how you will be able to know whether it is God's Spirit: everyone who declares that Jesus Christ became mortal man has the Spirit who comes from God." I John 4:2, TEV.

12. For this cause the king was angry and very furious, and commanded to destroy all the wise men of Babylon.

13. And the decree went forth that the wise men should be slain; and they sought Daniel and his fellows to be slain.

14. ¶ Then Daniel answered with counsel and wisdom to Arioch the captain of the king's guard, which was gone forth to slay the wise men of Babylon:

15. He answered and said to Arioch the king's captain, Why is the decree so hasty from the king? Then Arioch made the thing known to Daniel.

"Then Arioch." Arioch told Daniel of the king's dream and of his disappointment in his advisers. Daniel, at the risk of his life, entered the king's presence and asked for time to pray for knowledge of the dream and its meaning, PK493.

16. Then Daniel went in, and desired of the king that he would give him time, and that he would shew the king the interpretation.

17. Then Daniel went to his house, and made the thing known to Hananiah, Mishael, and Azariah, his companions:

18. That they would desire mercies of the God of heaven concerning this secret; that Daniel and his fellows should not perish with the rest of the wise men of Babylon.

"They would desire mercies." As Daniel and the three, convinced that God had providentially placed them within the king's court, by habit turned to Him, He honored their trust, PK493, 494.

19. ¶ Then was the secret revealed unto Daniel in a night vision. Then Daniel blessed the God heaven.

"Then Daniel blessed." His first work was to give thanks for being shown the dream and its meaning, PK494.

20. Daniel answered and said, Blessed be the name of God for ever and ever: for wisdom and might are his:

21. And he changeth the times and the seasons: he removeth kings, and setteth up kings: he giveth wisdom unto the wise, and knowledge to them that know understanding:

22. He revealeth the deep and secret things: he knoweth what is in the darkness, and the light dwelleth with him.

23. I thank thee, and praise thee, O thou God of my fathers, who hast given me wisdom and might, and has made known unto me now what we desired of thee: for thou has now made known unto us the king's matter.

24. ¶ Therefore Daniel went in unto Arioch, whom the king had ordained to destroy the wise men of Babylon: he went and said thus unto him; Destroy not the wise men of Babylon: bring me in before the king, and I will shew unto the king the interpretation.

25. Then Arioch brought in Daniel before the king in haste, and said thus unto him, I have found a man of the captives of Judah, that will make known unto the king the interpretation.

26. The king answered and said to Daniel, whose name was Belteshazzar, Art thou able to make known unto me the dream which I have seen, and the interpretation thereof?

"Art thou able?" Calmly Daniel took no credit for the revelation but honored God as the source of wisdom, PK494.

27. Daniel answered in the presence of the king, and said, The secret which the king hath demanded cannot the wise men, the astrologers, the magicians, the soothsayers, shew unto the king;

"Astrologers, magicians." See 1:20.

"Soothsayers" One claiming to possess the special gift of accurately determining the future of individuals and nations. By recourse to various occult arts they made their computations, divinations, and subtle prognostications, SDABD.

28. But there is a God in heaven that revealeth secrets, and maketh known to the king Nebuchadnezzar what shall be in the latter days. Thy dream, and the visions of thy head upon thy bed, are these;

"There is a God in heaven" By showing Nebuchadnezzar the future, God was endeavoring to convince him of his duty to heaven and of God's supreme power over all rulers, PK498.

29. As for thee, O king, thy thoughts came into thy mind upon thy bed, what should come to pass hereafter: and he that revealeth secrets maketh known to thee what shall come to pass.

30. But as for me, this secret is not revealed to me for any wisdom that I have more than any living, but for their sakes that shall make known the interpretation to the king, and that thou mightest know the thoughts of thy heart.

"But for their sakes." "In order that the meaning may be made known to the king and that you, O King, may understand the thoughts of your own heart," Berkeley Translation. "This secret has been revealed to me not because I am wise beyond all living men, but because your majesty is to know the interpretation and understand the thoughts which have entered your mind," NEB.

31. ¶ Thou, O king, sawest, and behold a great image. This great image, whose brightness was excellent, stood before thee; and the form thereof was terrible.

"A great image" This image not only represented the deterioration of earthly kingdoms in wealth, but also the increasing moral weakening of the people of these kingdoms, 4BC1168. It also showed the deterioration of religions, RH, Feb. 6, 1900

32. This image's head was of fine gold, his breast and his arms of silver, his belly and his thighs of brass,

33. His legs of iron, his feet part of iron and part of clay.

34. Thou sawest till that a stone was cut out without hands, which smote the image upon his feet that were of iron and clay, and brake them to pieces.

"Without hands." "Not by human hands," NEB, "By no human hand," RSV.

35. Then was the iron, the clay, the brass, the silver, and the gold, broken to pieces together, and became like the chaff of the summer threshingfloors; and the wind carried them away, that no place was found for them: and the stone that smote the image became a great mountain, and filled the whole earth.

"Broken to pieces together." Not separately. Jesus returns to earth at the close of the thousand years (see Revelation 20) and resurrects the wicked dead, whom Satan organizes and marches upon the New Jerusalem, surrounding the city. Now the executive judgment takes place, and as each sees his life passing in review before him like a closed-circuit television program, he realizes he had no excuse for refusing to surrender fully to Christ, and all, including Satan, bow the knee and confess that God was right and they were wrong, and are destroyed by fire, GC662–673.

36. ¶ This is the dream; and we will tell the interpretation thereof before the king.

37. Thou, O king, art a king of kings: for the God of heaven hath given thee a kingdom, power, and strength, and glory.

38. And wheresoever the children of men dwell, the beasts of the field and the fowls of the heaven hath he given into thine hand, and hath made thee ruler over them all. Thou art this head of gold.

39. And after thee shall arise another kingdom inferior to thee, and another third kingdom of brass, which shall bear rule over all the earth.

"And after thee." Babylon forgot God, crediting her prosperity to human effort alone, and was displaced, 4BC1168.

"And another." Medo-Persia was destroyed because they despised God's law, but the kingdoms that followed were increasingly more wicked and depraved, 4BC1168.

40. And the fourth kingdom shall be strong as iron: forasmuch as iron breaketh in pieces and subdueth all things: and as iron that breaketh all these, shall it break in pieces and bruise.

41. And whereas thou sawest the feet and toes, part of potters' clay, and part of iron, the kingdom shall be divided;

but there shall be in it of the strength of the iron, forasmuch as thou sawest the iron mixed with miry clay.

42. And as the toes of the feet were part of iron, and part of clay, so the kingdom shall be partly strong, and partly broken.

"Partly broken." "Brittle," RSV, NEB.

43. And whereas thou sawest iron mixed with miry clay, they shall mingle themselves with the seed of men: but they shall not cleave one to another, even as iron is not mixed with clay.

"Iron mixed with miry clay." The mixture of churchcraft and statecraft is thus represented, and God will execute judgment upon those who have thus nullified His law, 4BC1168, 1169.

44. And in the days of these kings shall the God of heaven set up a kingdom, which shall never be destroyed: and the kingdom shall not be left to other people, but it shall break in pieces and consume all these kingdoms, and it shall stand for ever.

45. Forasmuch as thou sawest that the stone was cut out of the mountain without hands, and that it brake in pieces the iron, the brass, the clay, the silver, and the gold; the great God hath made known to the king what shall come to pass hereafter: and the dream is certain, and the interpretation thereof sure.

"God hath made known." In the Bible we are shown that God is patiently working out His will behind the scenes, PK499, 500.

46. ¶ Then the king Nebuchadnezzar fell upon his face, and worshipped Daniel, and commanded that they should offer an oblation and sweet odours unto him.

47. The king answered unto Daniel, and said, Of a truth it is, that your God is a God of gods, and a Lord of kings, and a revealer of secrets, seeing thou couldest reveal this secret.

48. Then the king made Daniel a great man, and gave him many great gifts, and made him ruler over the whole

province of Babylon, and chief of the governors over all the wise men of Babylon.

49. Then Daniel requested of the king, and he set Shadrach, Meshach, and Abednego, over the affairs of the province of Babylon: but Daniel sat in the gate of the king.

"Over the affairs." The three companions of Daniel were made officials, but they humbly rejoiced to see God recognized, FE412, 413.

"The gate of the king." A court of justice, FE412.

DANIEL 3

1. Nebuchadnezzar the king made an image of gold, whose height was threescore cubits, and the breadth thereof six cubits: he set it up in the plain of Dura, in the province of Babylon.

"Nebuchadnezzar." In time the king backslid, PK503, 504.

"An image of gold." His counselors proposed that he make an image similar to the one in his dream, and the king decided to follow the suggestion, but to make the whole image of gold, thus declaring that his kingdom would not be displaced but would stand forever, PK504. This statue was about nine feet wide and ninety feet high, SL28. Sunday laws are exalted and regarded with the same reverence that the Babylonians had for this golden image, 4BC1169.

2. Then Nebuchadnezzar the king sent to gather together the princes, the governors, and the captains, the judges, the treasurers, the counsellors, the sheriffs, and all the rulers of the provinces, to come to the dedication of the image which Nebuchadnezzar the king had set up.

3. Then the princes, the governors, and captains, the judges, the treasurers, the counsellors, the sheriffs, and all the rulers of the provinces, were gathered together unto the dedication of the image that Nebuchadnezzar the king had set up; and they stood before the image that Nebuchadnezzar had set up.

4. Then an herald cried aloud, To you it is commanded, O people, nations, and languages,

5. That at what time ye hear the sound of the cornet, flute, harp, sackbut, psaltery, dulcimer, and all kinds of musick, ye fall down and worship the golden image that Nebuchadnezzar the king hath set up:

13

"Fall down and worship." *The very same counselors who had escaped death by Daniel's interpretation of the king's dream now enviously secured the death decree respecting the bowing down to the golden image, "Series A," page 161. It was understood by everyone that bowing to the image was an act of worship, and the three could give such worship to God only, PK507.*

6. And whoso falleth not down and worshippeth shall the same hour be cast into the midst of a burning fiery furnace.

7. Therefore at that time, when all the people heard the sound of the cornet, flute, harp, sackbut, psaltery, and all kinds of musick, all the people, the nations, and the languages, fell down and worshipped the golden image that Nebuchadnezzar the king had set up.

8. ¶ Wherefore at that time certain Chaldeans came near, and accused the Jews.

"Accused the Jews." *Jealous courtiers told the king of the disobedience of the Hebrew youth, PK506, 507. The idol, even though it was of solid gold, represented worshipping the king, and the young men could give such honor to none but God, 2SM312.*

9. They spake and said to the king Nebuchadnezzar, O king, live for ever.

10. Thou, O king, hast made a decree, that every man that shall hear the sound of the cornet, flute, harp, sackbut, psaltery, and dulcimer, and all kinds of musick, shall fall down and worship the golden image:

11. And whoso falleth not down and worshippeth, that he should be cast into the midst of a burning fiery furnace.

12. There are certain Jews whom thou hast set over the affairs of the province of Babylon, Shadrach, Meshack, and Abednego; these men, O king, have not regarded thee: they serve not thy gods, nor worship the golden image which thou hast set up.

"They serve not" To be called a fanatic is something a sincere child of God must expect, RH, March 14, 1893. Noah was called a fanatic by the people of his day, SR53, and the Pharisees declared that John the Baptist was a fanatic, DA275, 276.

13. ¶ Then Nebuchadnezzar in his rage and fury commanded to bring Shadrach, Meshach, and Abednego. Then they brought these men before the king.

14. Nebuchadnezzar spake and said unto them, Is it true, O Shadrach, Meshach, and Abednego, do not ye serve my gods, nor worship the golden image which I have set up?

15. Now if ye be ready that at what time ye hear the sound of the cornet, flute, harp, sackbut, psaltery, and dulcimer, and all kinds of musick, ye fall down and worship the image which I have made; well: but if ye worship not, ye shall be cast the same hour into the midst of a burning fiery furnace; and who is that God that shall deliver you out of my hands?

16. Shadrach, Meshack, and Abednego, answered and said to the king, O Nebuchadnezzar, we are not careful to answer thee in this matter.

"We are not careful." "We have no need to answer you on this matter. If there is a god who is able to save us from the blazing furnace, it is our God whom we serve, and He will save us from your power, O king; but if not, be it known to your majesty that we will neither serve your god nor worship the golden image that you have set up," NEB. Satan's rage at a martyr is the rage of a defeated enemy; the martyr is the victor, released by death from the persecutor's power, PP77. After one has taken his stand in wisdom and caution, he should never deviate from God's will, remaining as calm as a summer evening but as firm as the hills, "Letter 216," 1903. Jewish history had taught them that obedience brought prosperity and disobedience death and shame, PK508.

17. If it be so, our God whom we serve is able to deliver us from the burning fiery furnace, and he will deliver us out of thine hand, O king.

18. But if not, be it known unto thee, O king, that we will not serve thy gods, nor worship the golden image which thou has set up.

19. ¶ Then was Nebuchadnezzar full of fury, and the form of his visage was changed against Shadrach, Meshach, and Abednego: therefore he spake, and commanded that they should heat the furnace one seven times more than it was wont to be heated.

"His visage was changed." His face appeared as the face of a demon, and realizing that something unusual would occur in behalf of the youth, he ordered that his mightiest men take charge of them, 4BC1169.

20. And he commanded the most mighty men that were in his army to bind Shadrach, Meshach, and Abednego, and to cast them into the burning fiery furnace.

21. Then these men were bound in their coats, their hosen, and their hats, and their other garments, and were cast into the midst of the burning fiery furnace.

22. Therefore because the king's commandment was urgent, and the furnace exceeding hot, the flame of the fire slew those men that took up Shadrach, Meshach, and Abednego.

23. And these three men, Shadrach, Meshach, and Abednego, fell down bound into the midst of the burning fiery furnace.

24. Then Nebuchadnezzar the king was astonied, and rose up in haste, and spake, and said unto his counsellors, Did not we cast three men bound into the midst of the fire? They answered and said unto the king, True, O king.

25. He answered and said, Lo, I see four men loose, walking in the midst of the fire, and they have no hurt; and the form of the fourth is like the Son of God.

"They have no hurt." He who was with His faithful ones in the flames can also conquer our evil natures, MH90. The flames had no power to destroy in the presence of the God of ice and fire, PK509.

"Like the Son of God." Nebuchadnezzar, having been told by Daniel and his companions of Jesus, the promised Redeemer, recognized the One who was with them in the furnace, PK508, 509.

26. ¶ Then Nebuchadnezzar came near to the mouth of the burning fiery furnace, and spake, and said, Shadrach, Meshach, and Abednego, ye servants of the most high God, come forth, and come hither. Then Shadrach, Meshach, and Abednego, came forth of the midst of the fire.

"Come forth." They were unharmed, nothing having burned but their fetters, PK509, 510. Jesus was with them in the furnace, and all their associates were shown the faith which made their lives so noble, 4BC1170.

27. And the princes, governors, and captains, and the king's counsellors, being gathered together, saw these men, upon whose bodies the fire had no power, nor was an hair of their head singed, neither were their coats changed, nor the smell of fire had passed on them.

28. Then Nebuchadnezzar spake, and said, Blessed be the God of Shadrach, Meshach, and Abednego, who hath sent his angel, and delivered his servants that trusted in him, and have changed the king's word, and yielded their bodies, that they might not serve nor worship any god, except their own God.

29. Therefore I make a decree, That every people, nation, and language, which speak any thing amiss against the God of Shadrach, Meshach, and Abednego, shall be cut in pieces, and their houses shall be made a dunghill: because there is no other God that can deliver after this sort.

"I make a decree." Nebuchadnezzar exceeded his authority when he tried to make his subjects confess allegiance to God as he had done, for God leaves it to each to choose His service freely, PK510, 511.

"No other God that can deliver." Soon many will similarly suffer because of their loyalty to the Sabbath, and finally a world-wide death decree will be published against them, PK512. Printed decrees with a deadline will be circulated, allowing those who wish to, to kill Sabbath keepers after a certain time, EW282, 283. But supported by Jesus and His angels, the weakest saint will stand firm through the time of trouble, PK513.

30. Then the king promoted Shadrach, Meshach, and Abednego, in the province of Babylon.

DANIEL 4

1. Nebuchadnezzar the king, unto all people, nations, and languages, that dwell in all the earth; Peace be multiplied unto you.

2. I thought it good to shew the signs and wonders that the high God hath wrought toward me.

3. How great are his signs! and how mighty are his wonders! his kingdom is an everlasting kingdom, and his dominion is from generation to generation.

4. ¶ I Nebuchadnezzar was at rest in mine house, and flourishing in my palace:

5. I saw a dream which made me afraid, and the thoughts upon my bed and the visions of my head troubled me.

"I saw a dream." Pride over his achievement in making Babylon such a marvel of construction led God to send him a dream of warning, PK515.

6. Therefore made I a decree to bring in all the wise men of Babylon before me, that they might make known unto me the interpretation of the dream.

7. Then came in the magicians, the astrologers, the Chaldeans, and the soothsayers: and I told the dream before them; but they did not make known unto me the interpretation thereof.

"Magicians." See 1:20.

"Astrologers." See 1:20.

"Chaldeans." See 2:2.

"Soothsayers." See 2:27.

8. ¶ But at the last Daniel came in before me, whose name was Belteshazzar, according to the name of my god, and in whom is the spirit of the holy gods: and before him I told the dream, saying,

"Before him I told the dream." Again it was demonstrated that only those who reverence God can understand His workings, PK516.

9. O Belteshazzar, master of the magicians, because I know that the spirit of the holy gods is in thee, and no secret troubleth thee, tell me the visions of my dream that I have seen, and the interpretation thereof.

10. Thus were the visions of mine head in my bed: I saw, and behold, a tree in the midst of the earth, and the height thereof was great.

11. The tree grew, and was strong, and the height thereof reached unto heaven, and the sight thereof to the end of all the earth:

12. The leaves thereof were fair, and the fruit thereof much, and in it was meat for all: the beasts of the field had shadow under it, and the fowls of the heaven dwelt in the boughs thereof, and all flesh was fed of it.

13. I saw in the visions of my head upon my bed, and, behold, a watcher and an holy one came down from heaven;

14. He cried aloud, and said thus, Hew down the tree, and cut off his branches, shake off his leaves, and scatter his fruit: let the beasts get away from under it, and the fowls from his branches:

15. Nevertheless leave the stump of his roots in the earth, even with a band of iron and brass, in the tender grass of the field; and let it be wet with the dew of heavens, and let his portion be with the beasts in the grass of the earth:

16. Let his heart be changed from man's, and let a beast's heart be given unto him; and let seven times pass over him.

"Seven times." Seven years, AOT. For seven years the king remained humbled before the whole world, PK520.

17. This matter is by the decree of the watchers, and the demand by the word of the holy ones: to the intent that the living may know that the most High ruleth in the kingdom of men, and giveth it to whomsoever he will, and setteth up over it the basest of men.

18. This dream I king Nebuchadnezzar have seen. Now thou, O Belteshazzar, declare the interpretation thereof, forasmuch as all the wise men of my kingdom are not able to make known unto me the interpretation: but thou art able; for the spirit of the holy gods is in thee.

19. ¶ Then Daniel, whose name was Belteshazzar, was astonied for one hour, and his thoughts troubled him. The king spake, and said, Belteshazzar, let not the dream, or the interpretation thereof, trouble thee. Belteshazzar answered and said, My lord, the dream be to them that hate thee, and the interpretation thereof to thine enemies.

"Astonied for one hour." "For a time," Berkeley Translation. "For a moment," Moffatt. "Was dumbfounded for a moment, dismayed by his thoughts," NEB. "Was astonished and dismayed and stricken dumb for a while," AOT. Daniel realized the meaning of the dream, why it had been given, and its consequences, and he was startled, but he realized he must give Nebuchadnezzar the truth, whatever transpired to him as a result, PK517.

20. The tree that thou sawest, which grew, and was strong, whose height reached unto the heaven, and the sight thereof to all the earth,

21. Whose leaves were fair, and the fruit thereof much, and in it was meat for all; under which the beasts of the field dwelt, and upon whose branches the fowls of the heaven had their habitation:

22. It is thou, O king, that art grown and become strong: for thy greatness is grown, and reacheth unto heaven, and thy dominion to the end of the earth.

23. And whereas the king saw a watcher and an holy one coming down from heaven, and saying, Hew the tree down, and destroy it; yet leave the stump of the roots thereof in the earth, even with a band of iron and brass, in the tender grass of the field; and let it be wet with the dew of heaven, and let his portion be with the beasts of the field, till seven times pass over him;

24. This is the interpretation, O king, and this is the decree of the most High, which is come upon my lord the king:

25. That they shall drive thee from men, and thy dwelling shall be with the beasts of the field, and they shall make thee to eat grass as oxen, and they shall wet thee with the dew of heaven, and seven times shall pass over thee, till thou know that the most High ruleth in the kingdom of men, and giveth it to whomsoever he will.

26. And whereas they commanded to leave the stump of the tree roots; thy kingdom shall be sure unto thee, after that thou shalt have known that the heavens do rule.

27. Wherefore, O king, let my counsel be acceptable unto thee, and break off thy sins by righteousness, and thine iniquities by shewing mercy to the poor; if it may be a lengthening of thy tranquillity.

"A lengthening of thy tranquillity." "Perhaps your prosperity may be prolonged," Moffatt. "So may you enjoy peace of mind," NEB. Nebuchadnezzar, unconverted still, was impressed but a short while by his dream, and pride again took over until he even made light of his former concern, PK519.

28. ¶ All this came upon the king Nebuchadnezzar.

29. At the end of twelve months he walked in the palace of the kingdom of Babylon.

30. The king spake, and said, Is not this great Babylon, that I have built for the house of the kingdom by the might of my power, and for the honour of my majesty?

31. While the word was in the king's mouth, there fell a voice from heaven, saying, O king Nebuchadnezzar, to thee it is spoken; The kingdom is departed from thee.

32. And they shall drive thee from men, and thy dwelling shall be with the beasts of the field: they shall make thee to eat grass as oxen, and seven times shall pass over thee, until thou know that the most High ruleth in the kingdom of men, and giveth it to whomsoever he will.

33. The same hour was the thing fulfilled upon Nebuchadnezzar: and he was driven from men, and did eat grass as oxen, and his body was wet with the dew of heaven, till his hairs were grown like eagles' feathers, and his nails like birds' claws.

34. And at the end of the days I Nebuchadnezzar lifted up mine eyes unto heaven, and mine understanding returned unto me, and I blessed the most High, and I praised and honoured him that liveth for ever, whose dominion is an everlasting dominion, and his kingdom is from generation to generation:

"Mine understanding returned." Humbly the king admitted that God had rebuked him and publicly proclaimed God's mercy for restoring his sanity, PK520.

35. And all the inhabitants of the earth are reputed as nothing: and he doeth according to his will in the army of heaven, and among the inhabitants of the earth: and none can stay his hand, or say unto him, What doest thou?

36. At the same time my reason returned unto me; and for the glory of my kingdom, mine honour and brightness returned unto me; and my counsellors and my lords sought unto me; and I was established in my kingdom, and excellent majesty was added unto me.

37. Now I Nebuchadnezzar praise and extol and honour the King of heaven, all whose works are truth, and his ways judgment: and those that walk in pride he is able to abase.

"I Nebuchadnezzar." The king was converted and faithfully bore witness of God's mercy for the rest of his days, 4BC1170. This proclamation, Nebuchadnezzar's last act recorded in the Bible, showed that he had finally learned what every ruler needs to learn: true goodness is true greatness, PK521. Everyone who stays faithful to God to the end will experience similar heart humility, MS 15, 1888.

DANIEL 5

1. Belshazzar the king made a great feast to a thousand of his lords, and drank wine before the thousand.

2. Belshazzar, whiles he tasted the wine, commanded to bring the golden and silver vessels which his father Nebuchadnezzar had taken out of the temple which was in Jerusalem; that the king, and his princes, his wives, and his concubines, might drink therein.

3. Then they brought the golden vessels that were taken out of the temple of the house of God which was at Jerusalem; and the king, and his princes, his wives, and his concubines, drank in them.

4. They drank wine, and praised the gods of gold, and of silver, of brass, of iron, of wood, and of stone.

5. ¶ In the same hour came forth fingers of a man's hand, and wrote over against the candlestick upon the plaster of the wall of the king's palace: and the king saw the part of the hand that wrote.

"Fingers of a man's hand." It was God the Father's hand, the same hand that later tore the veil of the Jewish temple at Christ's expiring cry upon the cross, 5BC1109. All were silent in horrified terror, Belshazzar the most frightened of all, as they seemed to be appearing before God in judgment and their lives passed before them in panoramic view, PK524.

6. Then the king's countenance was changed, and his thoughts troubled him, so that the joints of his loins were loosed, and his knees smote one against another.

7. The king cried aloud to bring in the astrologers, the Chaldeans, and the soothsayers. And the king spake, and said to the wise men of Babylon, Whosoever shall read this writing, and shew me the interpretation thereof, shall be clothed with scarlet, and have a chain of gold about his neck, and shall be the third ruler in the kingdom.

"Astrologers." See 1:20.

"Chaldeans." See 2:2.

"Soothsayers." See 4:7.

"The third ruler." First ruler: Nabonidus, Nebuchadnezzar's stepson, not in Babylon at the time for some reason. Second ruler: Nabonidus' oldest son, Belshazzar, co-ruler with his father Nabonidus.

8. Then came in all the king's wise men: but they could not read the writing, nor make known to the king the interpretation thereof.

9. Then was king Belshazzar greatly troubled, and his countenance was changed in him, and his lords were astonied.

10. ¶ Now the queen by reason of the words of the king and his lords came into the banquet house: and the queen spake and said, O king, live for ever: let not thy thoughts trouble thee, nor let thy countenance be changed:

"The queen." Remembering how Daniel had interpreted the great image of Nebuchadnezzar's dream over fifty years before, the queen mother informed Belshazzar of the aged statesman, PK527, 528.

11. There is a man in thy kingdom, in whom is the spirit of the holy gods; and in the days of thy father light and understanding and wisdom, like the wisdom of the gods, was found in him; whom the king Nebuchadnezzar thy father, the king, I say, thy father, made master of the magicians, astrologers, Chaldeans, and soothsayers;

12. Forasmuch as an excellent spirit, and knowledge, and understanding, interpreting of dreams, and shewing of hard sentences, and dissolving of doubts, were found in the same

Daniel, whom the king named Belteshazzar: now let Daniel be called, and he will shew the interpretation.

13. Then was Daniel brought in before the king. And the king spake and said unto Daniel, Art thou that Daniel, which art of the children of the captivity of Judah, whom the king my father brought out of Jewry?

14. I have even heard of thee, that the spirit of the gods is in thee, and that light and understanding and excellent wisdom is found in thee.

"I have even heard of thee." Weak, foolish Belshazzar gloried in the power of the throne he had been allowed to share from his younger days, and although he had known of his grandfather's conversion, he had not been interested in making Nebuchadnezzar's choice his own, PK522, 523.

15. And now the wise men, the astrologers, have been brought in before me, that they should read this writing, and make known unto me the interpretation thereof: but they could not shew the interpretation of the thing:

16. And I have heard of thee, that thou canst make interpretations, and dissolve doubts: now if thou canst read the writing, and make known to me the interpretation thereof, thou shalt be clothed with scarlet, and have a chain of gold about thy neck, and shalt be the third ruler in the kingdom.

17. ¶ Then Daniel answered and said before the king, Let thy gifts be to thyself, and give thy rewards to another; yet I will read the writing unto the king, and make known to him the interpretation.

"Then Daniel answered." Daniel reminded the king of what he already knew and what he might have done, and showed him what the result of his indifference to God would soon be, PK529.

18. O thou king, the most high God gave Nebuchadnezzar thy father a kingdom, and majesty, and glory, and honour:

19. And for the majesty that he gave him, all people, nations, and languages, trembled and feared before him: whom he

would he slew; and whom he would he kept alive; and whom he would he set up; and whom he would he put down.

20. But when his heart was lifted up, and his mind hardened in pride, he was deposed from his kingly throne, and they took his glory from him:

21. And he was driven from the sons of men; and his heart was made like the beasts, and his dwelling was with the wild asses: they fed him with grass like oxen, and his body was wet with the dew of heaven; till he knew that the most high God ruled in the kingdom of men, and that he appointeth over it whomsoever he will.

22. And thou his son, O Belshazzar, hast not humbled thine heart, though thou knewest all this;

23. But hast lifted up thyself against the Lord of heaven; and they have brought the vessels of his house before thee, and thou, and thy lords, thy wives, and thy concubines, have drunk wine in them; and thou hast praised the gods of silver, and gold, of brass, iron, wood, and stone, which see not, nor hear, nor know; and the God in whose hand thy breath is, and whose are all thy ways, hast thou not glorified:

"Hast thou not glorified" God is glorified by fruit-bearing: John 15:8. Fruit is good works or deeds: Col. 1:10.

24. Then was the part of the hand sent from him; and this writing was written.

"Then was the part." "That is why that hand was sent from His very presence and why it wrote this inscription," NEB. The hand that had written the words was no longer to be seen, but the words were, as Daniel began to interpret them, PK530.

25. ¶ And this is the writing that was written, MENE, MENE, TEKEL UPHARSIN.

26. This is the interpretation of the thing: MENE; God hath numbered thy kingdom, and finished it.

27. TEKEL; Thou art weighed in the balances, and art found wanting.

"Thou art weighed in the balances." The phrase, "balances of the sanctuary," is referred to in the following references: ChS51, 3T30, TM439, 5T83, and 6T230, and suggests that character, conduct, motives, and moral worth are the things weighed. See note under Revelation 6:5.

28. PERES; Thy kingdom is divided, and given to the Medes and Persians.

29. Then commanded Belshazzar, and they clothed Daniel with scarlet, and put a chain of gold about his neck, and made a proclamation concerning him, that he should be the third ruler in the kingdom.

30. ¶ In that night was Belshazzar the king of the Chaldeans slain.

"In that night." Darius' nephew, Cyrus, commanding general of the armies of the Medes and Persians, besieged Babylon, PK523. The measure of the guilt of the Babylonian kingdom and its rulers was filled up on that night of revelry, and God could no longer protect them, PK530. Cyrus' soldiers had been penetrating the city's defenses after having diverted the Euphrates even while the feasting had been going on with the blasphemous drinking from the sacred vessels of God, PK531. Jeremiah had pictured this investment, comparing it to a caterpillar plague, Jer. 51:14.

31. And Darius the Median took the kingdom, being about threescore and two years old. 62 yrs old

DANIEL 6

1. It pleased Darius to set over the kingdom an hundred and twenty princes, which should be over the whole kingdom;

2. And over these three presidents; of whom Daniel was first: that the princes might give accounts unto them, and the king should have no damage.

"Daniel was first." Daniel's honors and his outstanding deportment aroused the jealousy of the king's nobles, PK539. As head of a cabinet of dishonest schemers, Daniel was in a difficult position. Spies could find nothing wrong, but Satan impressed the government leaders to use Daniel's devotion to spiritual things as a way of causing his condemnation, 4BC1171. Daniel did not claim to be sanctified, but he lived a dedicated life, free of any condemnation, SL32.

3. Then this Daniel was preferred above the presidents and princes, because an excellent spirit was in him; and the king thought to set him over the whole realm.

4. ¶ Then the presidents and princes sought to find occasion against Daniel concerning the kingdom; but they could find none occasion nor fault; forasmuch as he was faithful, neither was there any error or fault found in him.

"They could find none." Daniel lived so upright a life and did his work so well that his enemies were forced to concede that they could find no flaw, Ed56. The only accusation that could be made was that he prayed three times a day, SL32. God's people are to kneel also three times every day, 6T298.

5. Then said these men, We shall not find any occasion against this Daniel, except we find it against him concerning the law of his God.

6. Then these presidents and princes assembled together to the king, and said thus unto him, King Darius, live for ever.

7. All the presidents of the kingdom, the governors, and the princes, the counsellors, and the captains, have consulted together to establish a royal statute, and to make a firm decree, that whosoever shall ask a petition of any God or man for thirty days, save of thee, O king, he shall be cast into the den of lions.

8. Now, O king, establish the decree, and sign the writing, that it be not changed, according to the law of the Medes and Persians, which altereth not.

9. Wherefore king Darius signed the writing and the decree.

"Darius signed." By flattery the king was persuaded to sign the decree, ignorant of the real purpose behind it, PK540. The nobles gleefully congratulated themselves over having laid this trap for Daniel, SL33, but the nobles had themselves been trapped by evil angels, who, like them, feared that Daniel's good works would interfere with their plans of control, PK540.

10. ¶ Now when Daniel knew that the writing was signed, he went into his house; and his windows being open in his chamber toward Jerusalem, he kneeled upon his knees three times a day, and prayed, and gave thanks before his God, as he did aforetime.

"Now when Daniel." Daniel knew what would happen, but he felt he'd rather die than discontinue prayer, PK540, 541. By his actions he shows that no government has a right to dictate in matters of religion, and gives Christians an example of faithfulness, SL33, PK542. "Toward Jerusalem." Solomon, in his dedicatory prayer at the completion of the temple, asked that God would especially bless His people when they prayed toward the temple while in the lands of their captivity, I Kings 8:30,46–50.

11. Then these men assembled, and found Daniel praying and making supplication before his God.

"Found Daniel praying." Daniel prayed audibly, RH May 3, 1892. He considered prayer of such great importance that he would rather die than stop, 1T296. If one finds time to pray, God will find time to answer, RH, April 1, 1890. The sound of earnest prayer enrages Satan, who knows that he'll be defeated thereby, 1T295. Prayer is God's method of giving success in the battle with sin and in character growth, AA564. Secret prayer is a necessity for a soul to live, Ed258.

12. **Then they came near, and spake before the king concerning the king's decree; Hast thou not signed a decree, that every man that shall ask a petition of any God or man within thirty days, save of thee, O king, shall be cast into the den of lions? The king answered and said, The thing is true, according to the law of the Medes and Persians, which altereth not.**

13. **Then answered they and said before the king, That Daniel, which is of the children of the captivity of Judah, regardeth not thee, O king, nor the decree that thou hast signed, but maketh his petition three times a day.**

"That Daniel." As the nobles brought the accusation against Daniel before the king, he perceived at once that it had been resentment against Daniel, and not an interest in kingly honor that had motivated them, PK542, 543.

14. **Then the king, when he heard these words, was sore displeased with himself, and set his heart on Daniel to deliver him: and he laboured till the going down of the sun to deliver him.**

15. **Then these men assembled unto the king, and said unto the king, Know, O king, that the law of the Medes and Persians is, That no decree nor statute which the king establisheth may be changed.**

16. **Then the king commanded, and they brought Daniel, and cast him into the den of lions. Now the king spake and said unto Daniel, Thy God whom thou servest continually, he will deliver thee.**

"They brought Daniel." After the fall of Babylon, Darius ruled Medo-Persia two years and it was during that time that Daniel was thrust into the den of lions, RH, March 21, 1901. God allowed Daniel's enemies to triumph thus briefly to make Daniel's deliverance more marked, PK542, 543.

"He will deliver thee." One man, following right and duty, defeated Satan and honored and exalted the name of God, PK544. Every tendency toward evil in a human being will be subdued by the same Power that tamed the lions and cooled the flames of the fiery furnace, MH90.

17. And a stone was brought, and laid upon the mouth of the den; and the king sealed it with his own signet, and with the signet of his lords; that the purpose might not be changed concerning Daniel.

"A stone was brought." Every page of the Old Testament, be it history, or law, or prophetic utterance, is a type of Christ's and His experiences, DA211, so this was a symbolic prophecy of Christ's being put in the tomb after His crucifixion.

18. ¶ Then the king went to his palace, and passed the night fasting: neither were instruments of musick brought before him: and his sleep went from him.

19. Then the king arose very early in the morning, and went in haste unto the den of lions.

20. And when he came to the den, he cried with a lamentable voice unto Daniel: and the king spake and said to Daniel, O Daniel, servant of the living God, is thy God, whom thou servest continually, able to deliver thee from the lions?

21. Then said Daniel unto the king, O king, live for ever.

22. My God hath sent his angel, and hath shut the lions' mouths, that they have not hurt me; forasmuch as before him innocency was found in me; and also before thee, O king, have I done no hurt.

23. Then was the king exceeding glad for him, and commanded that they should take Daniel up out of the den.

So Daniel was taken up out of the den, and no manner of hurt was found upon him, because he believed in his God.

"No manner of hurt." Daniel in the den of lions was the same as when he was serving the king at court, so the one who is in touch with God will not be discouraged when things are unpleasant, PK545.

24. ¶ And the king commanded, and they brought those men which had accused Daniel, and they cast them into the den of lions, them, their children, and their wives; and the lions had the mastery of them, and brake all their bones in pieces or ever they came at the bottom of the den.

"The lions." "By order of the king Daniel's accusers were brought and thrown into the lions' pit with their wives and children, and before they reached the floor of the pit the lions were upon them and crunched them up, bones and all." NEB.

25. ¶ Then king Darius wrote unto all people, nations, and languages, that dwell in all the earth; Peace be multiplied unto you.

26. I make a decree, That in every dominion of my kingdom men tremble and fear before the God of Daniel: for he is the living God, and stedfast for ever, and his kingdom that which shall not be destroyed, and his dominion shall be even unto the end.

27. He delivereth and rescueth, and he worketh signs and wonders in heaven and in earth, who hath delivered Daniel from the power of the lions.

28 So this Daniel prospered in the reign of Darius, and in the reign of Cyrus the Persian.

"Daniel prospered." Daniel was prospered because he did the right thing, and we may be blessed in the same way if we have the same attitude, CH156. Daniel's life has been recorded to show us what one may become when in union with God, FE77. Strict self-control, undeviating in loyalty to God, Daniel was

greatly loved and admired by the officer who had been placed over him even while young, PK546.

DANIEL 7

1. In the first year of Belshazzar king of Babylon Daniel had a dream and visions of his head upon his bed: then he wrote the dream, and told the sum of the matters.

"A dream and visions." He didn't understand fully his own prophecies, but he was given assurance that at the end of earth's history they would be of significance. Satan leads many to believe that Daniel and Revelation are sealed, but there is here a clear promise that God will especially bless those who study them, PK47.

2. Daniel spake and said, I saw in my vision by night, and, behold, the four winds of the heaven strove upon the great sea.

"Winds." War: Jer. 25:29–33; 49:36; 51:1.

"Sea." "Peoples, and multitudes, and nations, and tongues," Rev. 17:15.

3. And four great beasts came up from the sea, diverse one from another.

"Beasts." Kingdoms, Daniel 7:23.

4. The first was like a lion, and had eagle's wings: I beheld till the wings thereof were plucked, and it was lifted up from the earth, and made stand upon the feet as a man, and a man's heart was given to it.

"Lion." Assyria and Babylon, Jer. 50:17.

"Eagle's wings." Chaldeans (Babylonians), Hab. 1:8; Deut. 28:49.

"As a man, and a man's heart." Fighting spirit lost, Jer. 51:30.

36

5. And behold another beast, a second, like to a bear, and it raised up itself on one side, and it had three ribs in the mouth of it between the teeth of it: and they said thus unto it, Arise, devour much flesh.

"Like to a bear." Medes; bearlike, cruel: Isa. 13:17,18.

"Three ribs." Lydia, Babylon, and Egypt, 4BC821.

6. After this I beheld, and lo another, like a leopard, which had upon the back of it four wings of a fowl; the beast had also four heads; and dominion was given to it.

"Four heads." After Alexander's death four divisions of his empire gradually came into prominence; Egypt, Seleucid, Macedonia, and Pergamum, which with its form of worship transported earlier from Babylon, was absorbed by Rome.

7. After this I saw in the night visions, and behold a fourth beast, dreadful and terrible, and strong exceedingly; and it had great iron teeth: it devoured and brake in pieces, and stamped the residue with the feet of it: and it was diverse from all the beasts that were before it; and it had ten horns.

"Horns." Powers, persecuting kingdoms: Zech. 1:18,19; PK581; Dan. 8:20,22.

8. I considered the horns, and, behold, there came up among them another little horn, before whom there were three of the first horns plucked up by the roots: and, behold, in this horn were eyes like the eyes of man, and a mouth speaking great things.

"Another little horn." Ten points that indicate that this horn is the papacy:

1–"Among them," verse 8, the nations of Europe, the "ten kings," verse 8.

2–"Another," verse 8, a kingdom also, "after them," verse 24.

3–"Three of the first horns plucked up by the roots," verse 8, because the three, Heruli, Ostrogoths, and Vandals, were Arian, didn't believe in the Trinity, and opposed the papacy that was to "subdue three kings," verse 24.

4–*"Eyes like the eyes of a man," verse 8, reasoning, looking to the future, laying long-range plans; "diverse from" the others, verse 24.*

5–*"Whose look was more stout than its fellows," verse 20, as it gained superiority over other kingdoms and world-wide influence.*

6–*"A mouth speaking great things," verse 8, "great words against the Most High," verse 25.*

7–*"Shall wear out the saints," verse 25, "made war with the saints and prevailed against them," verse 20.*

8–*"Think to change times and laws," verse 25, the principal one of which is the change of the Sabbath, which the papacy claims sole responsibility for having done, even asserting that the act is evidence of its power, GC446.*

9–*"Given into his hand until a time, times, and the dividing of time," verse 25, or "a year, two years, and half a year," American Translation, of prophetic time, from 538, when the Ostrogoths abandoned the siege of Rome and the Pope was freed from Arian control, until 1798, when France's General Berthier entered Rome, took the Pope prisoner, and declared the political rule of the papacy at an end, 1260 years of papal supremacy having come to a close.*

10–*"And they shall take away his dominion," verse 26, as was done by Berthier.*

9. ¶ I beheld till the thrones were cast down, and the Ancient of days did sit, whose garment was white as snow, and the hair of his head like the pure wool: his throne was like the fiery flame, and his wheels as burning fire.

"Cast down." Rather, "set in place" NEB, or "placed," RSV.

10. A fiery stream issued and came forth from before him: thousand thousands ministered unto him, and ten thousand

times ten thousand stood before him: the judgment was set, and the books were opened.

"The judgment was set." This is the investigative judgment of the professed people of God, which began in 1844, the judgment of the wicked taking place later, GC480.

"The books were opened." The book of life has the names recorded of all who have chosen the service of God, GC480, and the good deeds of the righteous, EW52. This work of investigative judgment began October 22, 1844, GC422, and will continue until the cases of all professing Christians have been examined, GC428.

11. I beheld then because of the voice of the great words which the horn spake: I beheld even till the beast was slain, and his body destroyed, and given to the burning flame.

12. As concerning the rest of the beasts, they had their dominion taken away: yet their lives were prolonged for a season and time.

13. I saw in the night visions, and, behold, one like the son of man came with the clouds of heaven, and came to the Ancient of days, and they brought him near before him.

"One like the son of man came with the clouds of heaven." This is not Christ's second coming to earth but His coming to the most holy place in the heavenly sanctuary for its cleansing from sin, GC426. as in the Temple service which is

"Came to the Ancient of days." When dressed in His robes as high priest, He entered the most holy place in a fiery chariot, accompanied by angels, there to minister before the throne of God, EW251.

14. And there was given him dominion, and glory, and a kingdom, that all people, nations, and languages, should serve him: his dominion is an everlasting dominion, which shall not pass away, and his kingdom that which shall not be destroyed.

a foreshadow of the heavenly Temple

"And there was given Him dominion, and glory, and a kingdom." He comes to the ancient of days to receive these, but they will not actually be given Him until His work as the high priestly Mediator is closed and He comes to earth the second time as a king, GC480.

15. ¶ I Daniel was grieved in my spirit in the midst of my body, and the visions of my head troubled me.

16. I came near unto one of them that stood by, and asked him the truth of all this. So he told me, and made me know the interpretation of the things.

17. These great beasts, which are four, are four kings, which shall arise out of the earth.

"Are four kings." That is, "kingdoms" verse 23.

18. But the saints of the most High shall take the kingdom, and possess the kingdom for ever, even for ever and ever.

"Saints." Those that "keep the commandments of God, and the faith of Jesus" Rev. 14:12.

19. Then I would know the truth of the fourth beast, which was diverse from all the others, exceeding dreadful, whose teeth were of iron, and his nails of brass; which devoured, brake in pieces, and stamped the residue with his feet;

20. And of the ten horns that were in his head, and of the other which came up, and before whom three fell; even of that horn that had eyes, and a mouth that spake very great things, whose look was more stout than his fellows.

21. I beheld, and the same horn made war with the saints, and prevailed against them;

22. Until the Ancient of days came, and judgment was given to the saints of the most High; and the time came that the saints possessed the kingdom.

"Judgment was given to the saints." Between the first resurrection, which takes place at Jesus' second coming for those who were true Christians, and the second resurrection, which raises

the wicked after the thousand-year period, the judgment of the *unrighteous takes place with the righteous saints of the Most* *High in charge, GC661.*

23. Thus he said, The fourth beast shall be the fourth kingdom upon earth, which shall be diverse from all kingdoms, and shall devour the whole earth, and shall tread it down, and break it in pieces.

24. And the ten horns out of this kingdom are ten kings that shall arise: and another shall rise after them; and he shall be diverse from the first, and he shall subdue three kings.

25. And he shall speak great words against the most High, and shall wear out the saints of the most High, and think to change times and laws: and they shall be given into his hand until a time and times and the dividing of time.

"Great words against the Most High." "The priest has the *power of the keys, or the power of delivering sinners from hell, of* *making them worthy of paradise, and of changing them from the* *slaves of Satan into the children of God, and God Himself is* *obliged to abide by the judgment of His priests. The Sovereign* *Master of the universe only follows the servant by confirming in* *heaven all that the latter decides on earth." "Dignities and* *Duties of the Priest," pp. 26,27, New York: Benziger Brothers,* *Printers to the Holy Apostolic See, 1888. "(Catholics owe)* *complete submission and obedience of will to the Church and to* *the Roman pontiff as to God Himself." Leo XIII, (encyclical)* *"Chief Duties of Christian Citizens." "The Pope is of so great* *dignity and so exalted that he is not a mere man, but as it were* *God, and the vicar of God. The Pope is of so great dignity and* *power that he can modify, explain, or interpret even divine* *laws." Translated from Lucius Ferraris, "Prompta* *Bibliotheca", Vol. VI, pp. 25–29, quoted in 4BC831.*

26. But the judgment shall sit, and they shall take away his dominion, to consume and to destroy it unto the end.

27. And the kingdom and dominion, and the greatness of the kingdom under the whole heaven, shall be given to the people of the saints of the most High, whose kingdom is an everlasting kingdom, and all dominions shall serve and obey him.

28. Hitherto is the end of the matter. As for me Daniel, my cogitations much troubled me, and my countenance changed in me: but I kept the matter in my heart.

DANIEL 8

1. In the third year of the reign of king Belshazzar a vision appeared unto me, even unto me Daniel, after that which appeared unto me at the first.

"After that which appeared unto me at the first." "Similar to my former vision," NEB.

2. And I saw in a vision; and it came to pass, when I saw, that I was at Shushan in the palace, which is in the province of Elam; and I saw in a vision, and I was by the river of Ulai.

3. Then I lifted up mine eyes, and saw, and, behold, there stood before the river a ram which had two horns: and the two horns were high; but one was higher than the other, and the higher came up last.

"Two horns." See 8:20.

4. I saw the ram pushing westward, and northward, and southward; so that no beasts might stand before him, neither was there any that could deliver out of his hand; but he did according to his will, and became great.

5. And as I was considering, behold, an he goat came from the west on the face of the whole earth, and touched not the ground: and the goat had a notable horn between his eyes.

"An he-goat." See 8:21.

6. And he came to the ram that had two horns, which I had seen standing before the river, and ran unto him in the fury of his power.

7. And I saw him come close unto the ram, and he was moved with choler against him, and smote the ram, and brake his two horns; and there was no power in the ram to stand before him, but he cast him down to the ground, and stamped upon

him: and there was none that could deliver the ram out of his hand.

8. Therefore the he goat waxed very great: and when he was strong, the great horn was broken; and for it came up four notable ones toward the four winds of heaven.

"Four notable ones." See 8:22.

"Toward the four winds of heaven." "The four quarters of heaven," NEB. Eventually Alexander's four leading generals became kings of different sections of his empire, Lysimachus taking the north, Ptolemy the south, Seleucus the east, and Cassander the west.

9. And out of one of them came forth a little horn, which waxed exceeding great, toward the south, and toward the east, and toward the pleasant land.

"A little horn." Rome's origin and progress, beginning small but eventually becoming "exceeding great." Since Medo-Persia is termed "great," verse 4, Antiochus Epiphanes, one of its minor kings, could not be called "exceeding great," as some interpreters do.

10. And it waxed great, even to the host of heaven; and it cast down some of the host and of the stars to the ground, and stamped upon them.

"The host of heaven." God's people, Israel. See 8:24.

11. Yea, he magnified himself even to the prince of the host, and by him the daily sacrifice was taken away, and the place of his sanctuary was cast down.

"Yea, he." Verses 11–14, paraphrased and amplified: "The papacy removed the daily from the thoughts of the people by establishing the sacrifice of the mass and a priesthood which made Christ's ministry unnecessary. So the abomination of desolation was set up in the papal system with the pope as its head. Then at the end of a 2300-year period, October 22, 1844, the heavenly sanctuary will be restored to its rightful position,

and those whose names are in the Book of Life will have their sins blotted out and they will be sealed."

"Daily." Hebrew, "tamid," continual or regular. "The regular offering," NEB. Both Rome, pagan and papal, "took away" the daily-pagan Rome by destroying the Jewish temple, and papal Rome by the substitution of the sacrifice of the mass and their priesthood, 4BC843.

12. And an host was given him against the daily sacrifice by reason of transgression, and it cast down the truth to the ground; and it practised, and prospered.

13. ¶ Then I heard one saint speaking, and another saint said unto that certain saint which spake, How long shall be the vision concerning the daily sacrifice, and the transgression of desolation, to give both the sanctuary and the host to be trodden under foot?

14. And he said unto me, Unto two thousand and three hundred days; then shall the sanctuary be cleansed.

"Then shall the sanctuary be cleansed." After the disappointment of October 22, 1844, a date that had been widely heralded as the time Jesus would return, further study revealed that instead of the earth's being cleansed by Christ's second coming, as had been believed and taught, the prophecy indicated: (a) Christ's closing work as High Priest in Heaven, (b) the completion of the atonement or blotting out of sin (Lev. 16:30; PP358), and (c) a preparing of God's people to be able to meet Christ at His coming, LS63. A false theory that Satan will try to introduce is that there is no sanctuary in Heaven, Ev224. For a clear and detailed explanation of the 2300-day prophecy, see GC324–329.

15. ¶ And it came to pass, when I, even I Daniel, had seen the vision, and sought for the meaning, then, behold, there stood before me as the appearance of a man.

16. And I heard a man's voice between the banks of Ulai, which called, and said, Gabriel, make this man to understand the vision.

17. So he came near where I stood: and when he came, I was afraid, and fell upon my face: but he said unto me, Understand, O son of man: for at the time of the end shall be the vision.

18. Now as he was speaking with me, I was in a deep sleep on my face toward the ground: but he touched me, and set me upright.

19. And he said, Behold, I will make thee know what shall be in the last end of the indignation: for at the time appointed the end shall be.

20. The ram which thou sawest having two horns are the kings of Media and Persia.

21. And the rough goat is the king of Grecia: and the great horn that is between his eyes is the first king.

22. Now that being broken, whereas four stood up for it, four kingdoms shall stand up out of the nation, but not in his power.

23. And in the latter time of their kingdom, when the transgressors are come to the full, a king of fierce countenance, and understanding dark sentences, shall stand up.

"Of fierce countenance and understanding dark sentences." *"Harsh and grim, a master of strategem,"* NEB. Rome.

24. And his power shall be mighty, but not by his own power: and he shall destroy wonderfully, and shall prosper, and practise, and shall destroy the mighty and the holy people.

25. And through his policy also he shall cause craft to prosper in his hand; and he shall magnify himself in his heart, and by peace shall destroy many: he shall also stand up against the Prince of princes; but he shall be broken without hand.

"Craft." *"Deceit,"* RSV; *"crafty designs,"* NEB; *"treachery,"* AOT; *"intrigues,"* Moffatt.

26. And the vision of the evening and the morning which was told is true: wherefore shut thou up the vision; for it shall be for many days.

27. And I Daniel fainted, and was sick certain days; afterward I rose up, and did the king's business; and I was astonished at the vision, but none understood it.

"None understood it." "No one could explain it," NEB.

DANIEL 9

1. In the first year of Darius the son of Ahasuerus, of the seed of the Medes, which was made king over the realm of the Chaldeans;

2. In the first year of his reign I Daniel understood by books the number of the years, whereof the word of the Lord came to Jeremiah the prophet, that he would accomplish seventy years in the desolations of Jerusalem.

"Understood by books." Letters sent by Jeremiah to the exiles in Babylon, letters sent by false prophets to them and to the rulers of Jerusalem, an account of the occurrences that transpired as a result, and some of Jeremiah's prophecies are recorded in Jeremiah, chapters 25 and 27–31. These were studied by Daniel more than sixty years after they had been written, 4BC1157, 1158.

3. ¶ And I set my face unto the Lord God, to seek by prayer and supplications, with fasting, and sackcloth, and ashes:

4. And I prayed unto the Lord my God, and made my confession, and said, O Lord the great and dreadful God, keeping the covenant and mercy to them that love him, and to them that keep his commandments;

"And I prayed." Many others, like Daniel, were praying for God to deliver His people as the time of captivity drew to a close, PK559. Daniel's example in prayer is for us. Just because God had promised deliverance, he did not sit idly and wait but sought God with fasting and prayer and confessed his and his people's sins, 4BC1172. We can be safe only by continually distrusting ourselves and depending upon Christ, COL156. Those failing to recognize their need of continually depending upon God will be defeated by sin, DA382. Everyone who is trying to grow in grace

needs the hour of quiet communion with God, nature, and his own heart, CH163. Not one is safe even for an hour without prayer, GC530.

"My confession." From verses 4–20 Daniel puts himself as an offender with Israel seventeen times.

5. We have sinned, and have committed iniquity, and have done wickedly, and have rebelled, even by departing from thy precepts and from thy judgments:

6. Neither have we hearkened unto thy servants the prophets, which spake in thy name to our kings, our princes, and our fathers, and to all the people of the land.

7. O Lord, righteousness belongeth unto thee, but unto us confusion of faces, as at this day; to the men of Judah, and to the inhabitants of Jerusalem, and unto all Israel, that are near, and that are far off, through all the countries whither thou has driven them, because of their trespass that they have trespassed against thee.

8. O Lord, to us belongeth confusion of face, to our kings, to our princes, and to our fathers, because we have sinned against thee.

9. To the Lord our God belong mercies and forgivenesses, though we have rebelled against him;

10. Neither have we obeyed the voice of the Lord our God, to walk in his laws, which he set before us by his servants the prophets.

11. Yea, all Israel have transgressed thy law, even by departing, that they might not obey thy voice; therefore the curse is poured upon us, and the oath that is written in the law of Moses the servant of God, because we have sinned against him.

12. And he hath confirmed his words, which he spake against us, and against our judges that judged us, by bringing upon us a great evil: for under the whole heaven hath not been done as hath been done upon Jerusalem.

13. As it is written in the law of Moses, all this evil is come upon us: yet made we not our prayer before the Lord our God, that we might turn from our iniquities, and understand thy truth.

14. Therefore hath the Lord watched upon the evil, and brought it upon us: for the Lord our God is righteous in all his works which he doeth: for we obeyed not his voice.

15. And now, O Lord our God, that hast brought thy people forth out of the land of Egypt with a mighty hand, and hast gotten thee renown, as at this day; we have sinned, we have done wickedly.

16. ¶ O Lord, according to all thy righteousness, I beseech thee, let thine anger and thy fury be turned away from thy city Jerusalem, thy holy mountain: because for our sins, and for the iniquities of our fathers, Jerusalem and thy people are become a reproach to all that are about us.

"Thy city Jerusalem, thy holy mountain." Prophecy applies references to Jerusalem or Zion to Israel, God's chosen people, as long as they remain in the Theocracy. But when her leaders and the mob at the trial of Christ declared, "We have no king but Caesar," John 19:15, the nation formally withdrew, and the Christian Church became Jerusalem, Zion, His people, I Pet. 2:5,9,10 and Heb. 12:22,23, and prophecies from that time on relating to Jerusalem or Zion are applied to the true church.

17. Now therefore, O our God, hear the prayer of thy servant, and his supplications, and cause thy face to shine upon thy sanctuary that is desolate, for the Lord's sake.

18. O my God, incline thine ear, and hear; open thine eyes, and behold our desolations, and the city which is called by thy name: for we do not present our supplications before thee for our righteousnesses, but for thy great mercies.

19. O Lord, hear; O Lord, forgive; O Lord, hearken and do; deter not, for thine own sake, O my God: for thy city and thy people are called by thy name.

20. ¶ And whiles I was speaking, and praying, and confessing my sin and the sin of my people Israel, and presenting my supplication before the Lord my God for the holy mountain of my God;

21. Yea, whiles I was speaking in prayer, even the man Gabriel, whom I had seen in the vision at the beginning, being caused to fly swiftly, touched me about the time of the evening oblation.

"Gabriel." Next in rank to Jesus, "His angel," that came to John on Patmos, DA234, took Satan's place in heaven, announced Jesus' birth to the shepherds at Bethlehem, and rolled the stone from Christ's tomb, DA780. He is the angel of prophecy that instructed the prophets, 3T80, DA99. He strengthened Christ in the Garden of Gethsemane, DA693, 5BC1123. He aided Cyrus, PK571, 572 and strengthened Darius the Mede, PK556. He also instructed Mary the mother of Jesus, DA81, 82, 98, and the father of John the Baptist, DA97, 98.

22. And he informed me, and talked with me, and said, O Daniel, I am now come forth to give thee skill and understanding.

23. At the beginning of thy supplications the commandment came forth, and I am come to shew thee; for thou art greatly beloved:

"Thou art greatly beloved." Daniel wrote this, PK547, but the Holy Spirit dictated it, II Peter 1:21, so he shouldn't be considered immodest or boastful for having to write what the Holy Spirit ordered.

24. Seventy weeks are determined upon thy people and upon thy holy city, to finish the transgression, and to make an end of sins, and to make reconciliation for iniquity, and to bring in everlasting righteousness, and to seal up the vision and prophecy, and to anoint the most Holy.

"To finish the transgression." Heb. *"kalah,"* *"to bring to completion,"* that is, the Jews would fill up their cup of iniquity by crucifying Jesus and persecuting His followers.

"Make an end of sins." This would be accomplished by Christ's death on the cross as an offering for sin and His ministry in the sanctuary to make an atonement or a blotting out of sin, PP358, thus *"making reconciliation for iniquity"* and bringing in *"everlasting righteousness."*

25. Know therefore and understand, that from the going forth of the commandment to restore and to build Jerusalem unto the Messiah the Prince shall be seven weeks, and threescore and two weeks: the street shall be built again, and the wall, even in troublous times.

"To restore and to build." Darius died about two years after Babylon's fall and Cyrus, his nephew, came to the throne. The seventy years of captivity that had been prophesied by Jeremiah, Jer. 25:11,12, were fulfilled at this time, and as Cyrus saw his name in the prophecy of Isa. 44:28 and the work he was to do, he was moved to make the decree for the rebuilding of Jerusalem, PK556, 557.

"The street shall be built again." God is in charge, and when the time came for Cyrus to do the work he had been named to do one hundred years before, the king was inspired to carry it out and free the captives, 4BC1175.

26. And after threescore and two weeks shall Messiah be cut off, but not for himself: and the people of the prince that shall come shall destroy the city and the sanctuary; and the end thereof shall be with a flood, and unto the end of the war desolations are determined.

"The people of the prince." Rome under Titus destroyed Jerusalem in 70 A.D. For a detailed picture of this, see the chapter, *"Destruction of Jerusalem,"* GC17–38.

27. And he shall confirm the covenant with many for one week: and in the midst of the week he shall cause the sacrifice

and the oblation to cease, and for the overspreading of abominations he shall make it desolate, even until the consummation, and summation, and that determined shall be poured upon the desolate.

"The overspreading of abominations." "And in the train of these abominations shall come an author of desolation; then in the end, what has been decreed concerning the desolation shall be poured out," NEB. "And instead of this there shall be an appalling abomination, till finally the appointed doom falls upon the sacreligious abomination," Moffatt. "While in their place there shall be a desolating abomination, till at the end the doom that is determined shall be poured out upon the desolating thing," American Translation. "Literally, 'wing.' Here the desolater is poetically pictured as being carried along upon the wing of abominations. This has reference in part at least to the horrors and atrocities that were perpetrated upon the Jewish nation by the Romans," 4BC855.

DANIEL 10

1. In the third year of Cyrus king of Persia a thing was revealed unto Daniel, whose name was called Belteshazzar; and the thing was true, but the time appointed was long: and he understood the thing, and had understanding of the vision.

"The time appointed was long." Chapters 10–12 summarize chapters 2, 7, 8–9 and cover the ground in more detail, emphasizing what shall be "in the latter days," 10:14.

2. In those days I Daniel was mourning three full weeks.

3. I ate no pleasant bread, neither came flesh nor wine in my mouth, neither did I anoint myself at all, till three whole weeks were fulfilled.

4. And in the four and twentieth day of the first month, as I was by the side of the great river, which is Hidekel;

"Hidekel." The visions Daniel saw there are especially for this time, being fulfilled now, and all will soon be completed, TM113.

5. Then I lifted up mine eyes, and looked, and behold a certain man clothed in linen, whose loins were girded with fine gold of Uphaz:

"A certain man." Jesus, accompanied by Gabriel, SL37, 4BC1173.

6. His body also was like the beryl, and his face as the appearance of lightning, and his eyes as lamps of fire, and his arms and his feet like in colour to polished brass, and the voice of his words like the voice of a multitude.

7. And I Daniel alone saw the vision: for the men that were with me saw not the vision; but a great quaking fell upon them, so that they fled to hide themselves.

"Saw the vision." The physical condition of a prophet in vision: (1) No strength, Dan. 10:8,16,17; (2) Strengthened, Dan. 10:18,19; (3) No breath, Dan 10:17; (4) Eyes open, Dan. 10:8; Num. 24:4,16.

8. Therefore I was left alone, and saw this great vision, and there remained no strength in me: for my comeliness was turned in me into corruption, and I retained no strength.

9. Yet heard I the voice of his words: and when I heard the voice of his words, then was I in a deep sleep on my face, and my face toward the ground.

10. ¶ And, behold, an hand touched me, which set me upon my knees and upon the palms of my hands.

11. And he said unto me, O Daniel, a man greatly beloved, understand the words that I speak unto thee, and stand upright: for unto thee am I now sent. And when he had spoken this word unto me, I stood trembling.

12. Then said he unto me, Fear not, Daniel: for from the first day that thou didst set thine heart to understand, and to chasten thyself before thy God, thy words were heard, and I am come for thy words.

13. But the prince of the kingdom of Persia withstood me one and twenty days: but, lo, Michael, one of the chief princes, came to help me; and I remained there with the kings of Persia.

"Withstood me." God's purposes meet with hindrances, as occurred when Cyrus was under the control of a superior evil force. Like Pharaoh he would not obey God, but Christ came to Gabriel's assistance, freeing Gabriel to go instruct Daniel, giving him the detailed prophecy of Daniel 11, 4BC1173.

"Remained there." Michael or Christ, 4BC1173.

14. Now I am come to make thee understand what shall befall thy people in the latter days: for yet the vision is for many days.

"Thy people in the latter days." Spiritual Israel, Christians.

15. And when he had spoken such words unto me, I set my face toward the ground, and I became dumb.

16. And, behold, one like the similitude of the sons of men touched my lips: then I opened my mouth, and spake, and said unto him that stood before me, O my lord, by the vision my sorrows are turned upon me, and I have retained no strength.

17. For how can the servant of this my lord talk with this my lord? for as for me, straightway there remained no strength in me, neither is there breath left in me.

18. Then there came again and touched me one like the appearance of a man, and he strengthened me,

19. And said, O man greatly beloved, fear not: peace be unto thee, be strong, yea, be strong. And when he had spoken unto me, I was strengthened, and said, Let my lord speak; for thou hast strengthened me.

20. Then said he, Knowest thou wherefore I come unto thee? and now will I return to fight with the prince of Persia: and when I am gone forth, lo, the prince of Grecia shall come.

"The prince of Persia." Cyrus under the control of one of the most powerful of the evil angels. 4BC1173.

21. But I will shew thee that which is noted in the scripture of truth: and there is none that holdeth with me in these things, but Michael your prince.

"None that holdeth with me." This shows that Gabriel holds a high position in Heaven, next to Christ, DA98, 99.

DANIEL 11

1. Also I in the first year of Darius the Mede, even I, stood to confirm and to strengthen him.

"Also I." Darius was given honor by having Gabriel himself come "to confirm and strengthen" him during his reign, PK556.

2. And now will I shew thee the truth. Behold, there shall stand up yet three kings in Persia; and the fourth shall be far richer than they all: and by his strength through his riches he shall stir up all against the realm of Grecia.

"Yet three kings." Darius died two years after Babylon's fall and was followed by his nephew Cyrus, in whose third year of rule Daniel received this vision, Dan. 10:1. The three kings following Cyrus were his son, Cambyses, who reigned around seven years and a half, PK572, and false Smerdis, termed Artaxerxes in Ezra 4:7, PK572, and Darius I Hystaspes.

"The fourth." Xerxes, Ahasuerus, or Creossus, who was quite proud of his wealth, Esther 1:4,6,7.

3. And a mighty king shall stand up that shall rule with great dominion, and do according to his will.

"A mighty king." Alexander, 336–323 B.C.

"Do according to his will." A clause that suggests that the ruler considers himself worthy of worship as a god. When Alexander founded the city of Alexandria in Egypt, he declared himself the successor to the Pharaohs, and his troops hailed him as a god, 4BC821. The clause also denotes universal dominion.

4. And when he shall stand up, his kingdom shall be broken, and shall be divided toward the four winds of heaven; and not to his posterity, nor according to his dominion which he

ruled: for his kingdom shall be plucked up, even for others beside those.

"Toward the four winds." See Dan. 7:6.

5. ¶ And the king of the south shall be strong, and one of his princes; and he shall be strong above him, and have dominion; his dominion shall be a great dominion.

"King of the south." Ptolemy I Soter.

"One of his princes." Seleucus I.

6. And in the end of years they shall join themselves together; for the king's daughter of the south shall come to the king of the north to make an agreement: but she shall not retain the power of the arm; neither shall he stand, nor his arm: but she shall be given up, and they that brought her, and he that begat her, and he that strengthened her in these times.

"The king's daughter." Bereniece, daughter of Ptolemy II Philadelphus.

"The king of the north." Antiochus II Theos.

"Neither shall he." Antiochus was poisoned by his first wife, Laodice.

"Nor his arm." Laodice also killed his son.

"She shall be given up." Laodice also killed Bereniece.

"They that brought her." Bereniece's Egyptian ladies in waiting were also slain.

7. But out of a branch of her roots shall one stand up in his estate, which shall come with an army, and shall enter into the fortress of the king of the north, and shall deal against them, and shall prevail:

"A branch of her roots." Ptolemy III Euergetes, Bereniece's brother, invaded Syria in revenge for her murder.

8. And shall also carry captives into Egypt their gods, with their princes, and with their precious vessels of silver and of

gold; and he shall continue more years than the king of the north.

9. So the king of the south shall come into his kingdom, and shall return into his own land.

"The king of the south." Seleucus Lias invaded the territory of the king of the north, but was defeated and returned home empty-handed.

10. But his sons shall be stirred up, and shall assemble a multitude of great forces: and one shall certainly come, and overflow, and pass through: then shall he return, and be stirred up, even to his fortress.

"His sons." Seleucus III and Antiochus III, sons of Seleucus II.

"And one." Antiochus III, "stirred up," added Palestine to his dominions.

11. And the king of the south shall be moved with choler, and shall come forth and fight with him, even with the king of the north: and he shall set forth a great multitude; but the multitude shall be given into his hand.

"The king of the south." Ptolemy IV, elated over recovering Palestine, tried to enter the most holy place, but "He was smitten from God with such confusion and terror that he was carried out of the place in a manner half dead. On this he departed from Jerusalem, filled with great wrath against the whole nation of the Jews for that which had happened to him in that place, and venting many threatenings against them for it." Prideaux, "Connection," 217 B.C.

"The king of the north: and he." Antiochus III.

"His hand." Ptolemy's hand, as Palestine was recaptured.

12. And when he hath taken away the multitude, his heart shall be lifted up; and he shall cast down many ten thousands; but he shall not be strengthened by it.

"He shall cast down many." Ptolemy IV slew 40,000 Jews in Alexandria.

"He shall not be strengthened by it." Egypt declined rapidly after this and he died at the age of thirty-seven.

13. For the king of the north shall return, and shall set forth a multitude greater than the former, and shall certainly come after certain years with a great army and with much riches.

"The king of the north." Antiochus XII.

14. And in those times there shall many stand up against the king of the south: also the robbers of thy people shall exalt themselves to establish the vision; but they shall fall.

"The king of the south." Antiochus Epiphanes.

"The robbers of thy people." "The men of violence among your own people," RSV; "some hotheads among your own people," NEB. The Maccabeans, a family of Jewish patriots who headed a successful revolt against Antiochus Epiphanes of Syria from 175 to 164 B.C.

"To establish the vision." The Maccabeans attempted to bring about the fulfillment of a dream the Jewish people had of deliverance from Gentile dominion.

"But they shall fall." In spite of victories over the Syrians and the ratification of the Jewish-Roman League of 161 B.C., the Jews became subject to Rome.

15. So the king of the north shall come, and cast up a mount, and take the most fenced cities: and the arms of the south shall not withstand, neither his chosen people, neither shall there be any strength to withstand.

"King of the north." Rome conquered Palestine, Syria, and Egypt in its march to world conquest.

16. But he that cometh against him shall do according to his own will, and none shall stand before him: and he shall stand in the glorious land, which by his hand shall be consumed.

"He that cometh against him." Pompey the Great, Roman general and statesman, member of the first triumvirate, invaded Egypt and Palestine in 63 BC.

"Do according to his own will." See Dan. 11:3.

"Shall be consumed." "And all of it shall be in his power," RSV; "it will come wholly into his power," NEB. Rome dominated Palestine.

17. He shall also set his face to enter with the strength of his whole kingdom, and upright ones with him; thus shall he do: and he shall give him the daughter of women, corrupting her: but she shall not stand on his side, neither be for him.

"He." Julius Caesar.

"Upright ones." The Jewish-Roman League of friendship, 161 B.C., did not spare the Jews from Roman conquest.

"The daughter of women." Heb., "a woman of eminence," Israel. See II Kings 19:21; Isa. 37:22; Jer. 6:2. Prophecy represents God's people, a church, as a woman.

"Corrupting her." The Jewish-Roman League was an act of spiritual adultery. See James 4:4.

"She shall not stand on his side." The Jewish people were the most bitter opponents of their rule that Rome had, DA 737.

18. After this shall he turn his face unto the isles, and shall take many: but a prince for his own behalf shall cause the reproach offered by him to cease; without his own reproach he shall cause it to turn upon him.

"The reproach offered by him to cease." The Roman Senate declared Julius Caesar commander-in-chief of the army, dictator for life, and a sacred person to be worshiped.

19. Then he shall turn his face toward the fort of his own land: but he shall stumble and fall, and not be found.

"He shall stumble and fall." He was assassinated in the Roman Senate in 44 B.C.

20. Then shall stand up in his estate a raiser of taxes in the glory of the kingdom: but within a few days he shall be destroyed, neither in anger, nor in battle.

"A raiser of taxes." Augustus Caesar. "And it came to pass in those days, that there went out a decree from Caesar Augustus, that all the world should be taxed." Luke 2:1. He is the one responsible for bringing to Bethlehem the mother of Jesus, DA44.

"In the glory of the kingdom." Augustus established the Roman Empire and reigned during Rome's "Golden Age."

"Destroyed neither in anger, nor in battle." He reigned forty years, dying peaceably in bed, 14 A.D.

21. And in his estate shall stand up a vile person, to whom they shall not give the honour of the kingdom: but he shall come in peaceably, and obtain the kingdom by flatteries.

"A vile person." Tiberius Caesar was an eccentric, misunderstood, unloved person, lightly esteemed or despised. He was a stepson of Augustus only, and not a genuine heir to the throne.

22. And with the arms of a flood shall they be overthrown from before him, and shall be broken; yea, also the prince of the covenant.

"The arms of a flood." Tiberius was successful in military campaigns.

"The prince of the covenant." Jesus was crucified during the reign of Tiberius, and on the order of his procurator or governor, Pontius Pilate in 31 A.D.

23. And after the league made with him he shall work deceitfully: for he shall come up, and shall become strong with a small people.

"And after the league." A flashback to the Jewish-Roman League of 161 B.C., tracing the growth of Rome.

24. He shall enter peaceably even upon the fattest places of the province; and he shall do that which his fathers have not

done, nor his fathers' fathers; he shall scatter among them the prey, and spoil, and riches: yea, and he shall forecast his devices against the strong holds, even for a time.

"He shall scatter." Rome was the first nation in history to gain dominion by exploiting the hopes of oppressed people. She also received kingdoms peaceably by the custom of kings leaving by legacy their provinces to the Romans, who gave protection and peace. Her own soldiers were rewarded well; for example, Caracalla, emperor from 211 to 217 A.D., increased soldiers' pay by one-half and gave them lavish donations.

"Even for a time." A "time" or year prophetically would be 360 years. From 31 B.C., the Battle of Actium, in which Augustus won over the forces of Cleopatra and Antony, to 330 A.D., when the seat of empire was moved from Rome to Constantinople, covers this period of time.

25. And he shall stir up his power and his courage against the king of the south with a great army; and the king of the south shall be stirred up to battle with a very great and mighty army; but he shall not stand: for they shall forecast devices against him.

"And he shall stir." Augustus, now the king of the north, prepared for an engagement against Antony, his brother-in-law, who had taken Cleopatra as his mistress and was attempting to establish himself as the master of the eastern world, the king of the south. "He shall not stand." In a naval battle between the two, Antony was defeated, his army deserted to Augustus, and he took his own life.

26. Yea, they that feed of the portion of his meat shall destroy him, and his army shall overflow: and many shall fall down slain.

"They that feed." Describes the desertion of Antony's army.

27. And both these kings' hearts shall be to do mischief, and they shall speak lies at one table; but it shall not prosper: for yet the end shall be at the time appointed.

"And both." As brothers-in-law they had had close associa-tion, but yet there had come intrigue and treachery.

28. Then shall he return into his land with great riches; and his heart shall be against the holy covenant; and he shall do exploits, and return to his own land.

"Then shall he return." Two returns are here suggested. The first was Augustus' return after the overthrow of Antony in the Battle of Actium, 31 A.D. The second, "when he shall do exploits," may describe Titus' return after the destruction of Jerusalem, 70 A.D. The Jewish war itself, which preceded Jerusalem's destruction, lasted seven years in which 1,462,000 died. The five-month siege of Jerusalem saw 110,000 killed and netted 97,000 prisoners for Rome.*

29. At the time appointed he shall return, and come toward the south; but it shall not be as the former, or as the latter.

"Toward the south." Pharoah's, "I know not Jehovah," represents atheism, and so Egypt, the king of the south, stands for the spirit of atheism which gradually began to creep into the Christian Church as a usurper began to exalt "himself above all that is called God," II Thess. 2:4.*

30. ¶ For the ships of Chittim shall come against him: there-fore he shall be grieved, and return, and have indignation against the holy covenant: so shall he do; he shall even return, and have intelligence with them that forsake the holy covenant.

"The ships of Chittim." In Daniel's day Chittim referred geographically to the lands and peoples of the west; Vandals and foreign aggressors plagued Rome, causing her decline and fall, leading to the establishment of a new king of the north: "Long ages ago when Rome through the neglect of the western emper-ors was left to the mercy of the barbarous hordes, the Romans turned to one figure for aid and protection and asked him to rule them; and thus commenced the temporal sovereignty of the popes. And meekly stepping to the throne of Caesar, the vicar of Christ took up the scepter to which the emperors and kings of*

Europe were to bow in reverence through so many ages." James F. Conroy, American Catholic Quarterly Review, April, 1911.

"Out of the ruins of political Rome arose the great moral empire in the giant form of the Roman Church." A. C. Flick, The Rise of the Mediaeval Church, p. 150.

"(The papacy was but) the ghost of the deceased Roman Empire, crowned and seated upon the grave thereof." Thomas Hobbes, English historian.

"Against the holy covenant." The ten commandments, Deut. 4:13; Ex. 34:28. In reply to a letter inquiring if the Roman Catholic Church changed the Sabbath and considered the change as a mark of her authority, Cardinal Gibbons replied through The Catholic Mirror, his official organ, "Of course the Catholic Church claims that the change was her act. It could not have been otherwise, as none in those days would have dreamed of doing anything in matters spiritual and religious without her, and the act is a mark of her ecclesiastical power and authority in religious matters." September 23, 1893.

"Have intelligence." Clovis, king of the Franks, established the power of the priesthood in 508.

31. And arms shall stand on his part, and they shall pollute the sanctuary of strength, and shall take away the daily sacrifice, and they shall place the abomination that maketh desolate.

"Pollute the sanctuary." Rome's substitution of the mass and the confessional in place of Jesus' ministry as our Priest in the sanctuary, Heb. 2:17; 4:14–16, taking away "the daily" or continual intercession, Heb. 7:25.

32. And such as do wickedly against the covenant shall he corrupt by flatteries: but the people that do know their God shall be strong, and do exploits.

"He." The papacy.

"Flatteries." Hebrew, "smooth, slippery things." In order to be more acceptable to the world, the church accepted the rule of the Bishop of Rome, Satan's representative, GC50.

"People that do know their God." Waldenses. See GC61–78.

33. And they that understand among the people shall instruct many: yet they shall fall by the sword, and by flame, by captivity, and by spoil, many days.

"By captivity." During the period of papal persecution, God's true church was just as much in captivity as Israel had been in Babylon, PK714.

"Many days." When the Bishop of Rome was designated as supreme ruler in 538 by Emperor Julian until 1798 when France's General Berthier took the pope prisoner, marks the period of papal supremacy, a 1260-year period.

34. Now when they shall fall, they shall be holpen with a little help: but many shall cleave to them with flatteries.

"Holpen." Waldenses and Albigenses found refuge in the mountains, while others fled to other countries or the lands of the New World.

"The earth helped the woman." The true church, Rev. 12:16.

"Many shall cleave to them with flatteries." The Reformation had many merely professed friends who proved to be enemies.

35. And some of them of understanding shall fall, to try them, and to purge, and to make them white, even to the time of the end: because it is yet for a time appointed.

"Some of them of understanding shall fall." Many leaders, such as Huss and Jerome and others, were martyred. "Some of these leaders will themselves fall victims for a time so they may be tested, refined, and made shining white." NEB. "The time of the end." The time in which we are now living. 5T10.

36. And the king shall do according to his will; and he shall exalt himself, and magnify himself above every god, and shall speak marvellous things against the God of gods, and shall

prosper till the indignation be accomplished: for that that is determined shall be done.

"And the king." "Here the pope is clearly pictured." Luther. Froom, Prophetic Faith of Our Fathers, vol. 2, p. 270.

"According to his will." See Dan. 11:3.

"Indignation be accomplished." That is, he shall continue in a prosperous state until the seven last plagues have been completed. That "indignation" means the seven last plagues, see Rev. 14:10 and 15:1. Paul declares that the papacy, "the man of sin," will remain in existence until Christ's second coming, GC579.

37. Neither shall he regard the God of his fathers, nor the desire of women, nor regard any god: for he shall magnify himself above all.

"The desire of women." A woman's desire for a home and husband, Gen. 3:16, is disregarded in the vows of celibacy nuns are forced to take. See I Tim. 4:1–3. "He shall magnify himself above all." See II Thess. 2:3,4.

38. But in his estate shall he honour the God of forces: and a god whom his fathers knew not shall he honour with gold, and silver, and with precious stones, and pleasant things.

"In his estate." That is, in God's place.

"The god of fortresses." The saints with their relics and images as protectors against various dangers.

"A god whom his fathers knew not." Mary worship or wafer worship, called the "host," a Latin word meaning a victim or sacrifice. It is taught that when the priest pronounces, "This is My body," the wafer becomes the actual body and blood of Christ, the process being termed transubstantiation.

39. Thus shall he do in the most strong holds with a strange god, whom he shall acknowledge and increase with glory: and he shall cause them to rule over many, and shall divide the land for gain.

"He shall cause them to rule." See Alphonsus de Liguori on *"Dignity and Duties of the Priest"* at Dan. 7:25.

"Divide the land." Pope Alexander VI in 1493 divided the New World between Spain and Portugal. Bishoprics and church offices were sold, the practice of simony being quite common.

40. And at the time of the end shall the king of the south push at him: and the king of the north shall come against him like a whirlwind, with chariots, and with horsemen, and with many ships; and he shall enter into the countries, and shall overflow and pass over.

"At the time of the end." The time since 1798.

"Shall the king of the south push." Not to be understood as a weak feint but complete conquest, as the ram *"pushed"* in its conquest, Dan. 8:4;. France's revolutionary atheistical government, resembling Pharaoh's, *"I know not the Lord,"* now representing Egypt's ways, becomes the king of the south, GC269, and General Berthier's taking the pope prisoner represents the complete conquest of the king of the north by the king of the south.

The papacy *"The king of the north."* Differing from a new idea that Elder Uriah Smith had presented that the king of the north was Turkey, Elder James White wrote in the Review and Herald of Nov. 29, 1877, *"Let us take a brief view of the line of prophecy four times spanned in the book of Daniel. It will be admitted that the same ground is passed over in chapters 2,7,8, and 11. We first pass down the great image of Chapter 2, where Babylon, Persia, Greece, and Rome are represented by the gold, the silver, the brass, and the iron. All agree that these feet are not Turkish but Roman. And as we pass down to the lion, the bear, the leopard, and the beast with ten horns, representing the same as the great image, again all will agree that it is not Turkey that is cast into the burning flame, but the Roman beast. So of chapter 8, all agree that the little horn that stood up against the Prince of princes is not Turkey but Rome. In all these thus far, Rome is the last form of government mentioned. Now comes the point in the argument upon which very much depends. Does the 11th chapter of the prophecy of Daniel cover the ground measured by chapters 2, 7, and 8? If so, then the last power mentioned in that chapter is Rome."*

"Shall come." People unite against God's people under the leadership of the papacy, 7T182.

"Against him." The king of the south, whose atheistical government is now represented by the communistic powers. "All Soviet citizens—not just the Jews—suffer from the Soviet government's policy of militant atheism." Time, Nov. 22, 1971.

41. He shall enter also into the glorious land, and many countries shall be overthrown: but these shall escape out of his hand, even Edom, and Moab, and the chief of the children of Ammon.

"The glorious land." When at Christ's trial before Pilate, "The chief priests answered, We have no king but Caesar," John 19:15, the Jewish people by their own decision chose not to continue as God's people, DA738, and prophecies beyond the cross dealing with Zion, Jerusalem, the "glorious land," or "My people," now have a spiritual and world-wide application which is applicable to God's true church, I Pet. 2:5,10; Matt. 21:43. The papacy, the king of the north, unites the forces of the world under his leadership to persecute the people of God, 7T182.

"Countries." A supplied word. "And tens of thousands shall fall," RSV. Trials will cause members of the church to withdraw from fellowship and apostatize, 6T400, 401, one of the causes of the "shaking." Other causes are false doctrine, TM112, and the straight message for Laodiceans, EW270.

"Edom, and Moab, and Ammon." These relatives of Israel may be compared to church dropouts, for whom a special effort will be made at this time with good results, 6T401.

42. He shall stretch forth his hand also upon the countries: and the land of Egypt shall not escape.

"The land of Egypt." Symbolic Egypt, Rev. 11:8, signifying organized atheism or open anti-Christianity, is well represented in international communism.

43. But he shall have power over the treasures of gold and of silver, and over all the precious things of Egypt: and the Libyans and the Ethiopians shall be at his steps.

"Libyans and Ethiopians." These persecutors of literal Israel in former times are representatives of armed forces "at his steps" or orders of the king of the north to persecute spiritual Israel.

44. But tidings out of the east and out of the north shall trouble him: therefore he shall go forth with great fury to destroy, and utterly to make away many.

"Tidings." The latter rain, loud cry, that calls God's people to separate from Babylon, the fallen apostate churches, Rev. 18:1–5, attended with great power and miracles, worldwide in scope, GC611, 612; EW271.

"Out of the east." A message powered by angels, who come from the east, Rev. 7:2,3.

"Out of the north." The loud cry message comes from God's throne, located in the north, Isa. 14:13; Psalm 48:2.

"Shall trouble him." Those who stubbornly refuse to heed God's final warning to separate from Babylon will be exasperated by its power and success, EW278; GC607.

"Therefore." Armed men, impelled by evil angels, attempt to annihilate the people of God scattered throughout the world in one concerted effort, but they are prevented by God's intervention, GC635, 636.

45. And he shall plant the tabernacles of his palace between the seas in the glorious holy mountain; yet he shall come to his end, and none shall help him.

"Plant the tabernacles of his palace." A military term suggesting a campaign, as is described in the above-mentioned reference in GC635, 636.

"Between the seas in the glorious holy mountain." Spiritual Jerusalem, His church, God's people, are the intended victims in this campaign of attempted extermination, but the intense blackness of the fifth plague, Rev. 16:10, covering the world, the *"seat"* (Gr. *"region"*) of the beast, stops the march of death and *"dries up"* the River Euphrates, sixth plague, Rev. 16:12, the persecuting power which a river symbolizes (Isa. 8:7), which is followed by the voice of God in the seventh plague, saying, *"It is done,"* Rev. 16:17.

"Shall come to his end, and none shall help him." The kings of the earth, the merchants and the shipmasters all *"stand afar off"* mourning the fall of Babylon but unable to help, Rev. 18:9–19.

DANIEL 12

1. And at that time shall Michael stand up, the great prince which standeth for the children of thy people: and there shall be a time of trouble, such as never was since there was a nation even to that same time: and at that time thy people shall be delivered, every one that shall be found written in the book.

"And at that time." The time that he plants, encamps against God's Remnant people in an attempt to destroy them.

"Shall Michael stand up." Michael is Christ: Jude 9; I Thess. 4:16,17; John 5:28,29. When He shall "stand up," reign (Dan. 11:2), exchanging His high-priestly robes for His kingly garments just before His second coming, a great time of trouble takes place in which the seven last plagues are poured out, Rev. 16.

"At that time." The time that the king of the north comes to his end as he is destroyed by the brightness and glory of Jesus' second coming, II Thess. 1:7,8, and God's people are taken up into the clouds with Him, I Thess. 4:16,17.

2. And many of them that sleep in the dust of the earth shall awake, some to everlasting life, and some to shame and everlasting contempt.

"And many." Not all are raised in this special resurrection that takes place just before Jesus appears in the clouds, but "many." There are three groups: (1) All those who died in the faith of the message that has been proclaimed since 1844, the Third Angel's Message; (2) those who took part in Christ's crucifixion, "that pierced Him," Rev. 1:7; (3) the outstanding persecutors of the people of God through the ages, GC637.

3. And they that be wise shall shine as the brightness of the firmament; and they that turn many to righteousness as the stars for ever and ever.

"And they that be wise." "Those who are teachers shall then shine as the brightness of the firmament, and those who turned many to righteousness as the stars for ever and ever," Berkeley Version. One soul saved for heaven is of greater value than ten thousand of our worlds, RH, August 1, 1880. The saving of souls, the winning of men from sin, is the very highest science, the greatest work that one may strive to do, MH398, and should be the life work of every one who claims to be a Christian, 4T53.

4. But thou, O Daniel, shut up the words, and seal the book, even to the time of the end: many shall run to and fro, and knowledge shall be increased.

"Seal the book." Daniel was to be sealed, its prophecies not to be understood until after the time of the end, 1798, GC356. These words do not apply to the book of Revelation, a "revealing," an opening of Daniel, 2SM109.

"Many shall run to and fro." Joseph Wolff reveals that this is a Hebrew expression for observing and thinking about time, GC360. "Then many shall run to and fro and search anxiously (through the Book), and knowledge (of God's purposes as revealed by His prophets) shall be increased and become great," Amplified Bible.

6. And one said to the man clothed in linen, which was upon the waters of the river, How long shall it be to the end of these wonders?

"And one said." Daniel, who twice asked, "How long shall it be?" TM114. "The man clothed in linen." Christ, RH, March 7, 1889.

7. And I heard the man clothed in linen, which was upon the waters of the river, when he held up his right hand and his left hand unto heaven, and sware by him that liveth for ever that it shall be for a time, times, and an half; and when he shall

have accomplished to scatter the power of the holy people, all these things shall be finished.

"Time, times and an half." The 1260-year period of papal supremacy, 538–1798.

8. And I heard, but I understood not: then said I, O my Lord, what shall be the end of these things?

9. And he said, Go thy way, Daniel: for the words are closed up and sealed till the time of the end.

10. Many shall be purified, and made white, and tried; but the wicked shall do wickedly: and none of the wicked shall understand; but the wise shall understand.

11. And from the time that the daily sacrifice shall be taken away, and the abomination that maketh desolate set up, there shall be a thousand two hundred and ninety days.

"And from the time." Literal: "And from the time of the taking away of the continual, even in order to set up the abomination."

"A thousand two hundred and ninety days." The 1843 chart, used by the Millerites during the 1830s, was created under the guidance of God and the dates were those that met His approval and were not to be changed, EW74. This chart declares that the taking away of the daily or continual sacrifice and the setting up of the abomination as having taken place in 508, the baptism of Clovis, king of the Franks. The support of Clovis established the priesthood of the Roman Catholic Church. The 1,290-year period extends to 1798 the "time of the end," when the book of Daniel was to be unsealed by study of students of prophecy in comparison with the Revelation.

12. Blessed is he that waiteth, and cometh to the thousand three hundred and five and thirty days.

"The thousand three hundred and five and thirty days." Again following the guidance of the 1843 Millerite chart with its beginning date of 508, 1335 takes us to 1843, a time when faithful

believers were expecting Christ's return to earth and were blessed as they cherished this hope.

13. But go thou thy way till the end be: for thou shalt rest, and stand in thy lot at the end of the days.

"Stand in thy lot." Daniel was given assurance that his prophecies would be of special significance in the final days of this world's history, PK547.

ENCOURAGEMENT FOR THE STUDY OF THE REVELATION

In the Revelation there was unfolded scene after scene of interest in the experience of the people of God, and the history of the church was foretold to the very close of time. In figures and symbols subjects of vast importance were presented to John which he was to record that the people of God living in his age and in furture ages might have an intelligent understanding of the perils and conflicts before them. This revelation was given for the guidance and comfort of the church throughout the Christian dispensation, AA583.

In the Revelation are portrayed the deep things of God. The very name given to its inspired pages, the Revelation, contradicts the statement that this is a sealed book. A revelation is something revealed, AA584.

The instruction to be communicated to John was so important that Christ came from heaven to give it to His servant, telling him to send it to the churches, 7BC953.

If God's people realized the nearness of the events portrayed in the Revelation, a reformation would be wrought in all churches, TM118.

OUTLINE OF REVELATION

Revelation's messages have been given in order, 8T302.

Chapter 1–John is instructed to write the things he is to be shown, and he does this by first presenting a preview, the Seven Churches, followed by specific details.

Chapters 2, 3–Seven Christian churches in Asia which have similar characteristics with the Christian Church at different periods of history receive warnings and/or commendations, starting with the apostolic period, Ephesus, to the time of the second coming of Christ, Laodicea.

Chapters 4, 5, 6, 8:1–The first seal of the seven is opened at the start of the Investigative Judgment, October 22, 1844, and they continue also to the second coming.

Chapter 7–The question asked in 6:17, "Who shall be able to stand?" is answered by this chapter's presentation of the 144,000 and the redeemed host of all the ages, 1T78.

Chapters 8, 9, 11:15–Seven warnings, trumpets (Joel 2:1), come just before the opening of the seventh seal, Christ's Second Coming, to prepare God's people for the "little time of trouble," the first four trumpets covering this period just before the close of probation, Chapter 8; and "the great time of trouble," falling of the seven last plagues, Chapter 9 and 11:15–19.

Chapter 10–A flashback shows Jesus, "Mighty Angel," revealing the great disappointment suffered by Millerites on October 22, 1844, and urging an "eating" of Daniel in order to be strengthened to stand through more conflicts to come.

Chapter 11–Jesus shows what can happen when a whole nation, France, rejects the Bible, the French Revolution resulting.

Chapter 12–To show the course of history leading up to Christ's taking the rulership of earth, shown in 11:15–19, a flashback outlines Satan's rebellion, Christ's birth, and the persecution of His followers, with finally an all-out war against the Remnant by Satan, the dragon.

Chapter 13–Satan is assisted in this final war by a union of two ecclesiastical powers, the papal beast and the animal with lamb-like horns, that attempt to force their mark, Sunday-keeping enforced by laws which forbid Sabbath-keeping, upon all.

Chapter 14–The 144,000 will not receive this mark and are sealed, three angels' messages, warning against this union, Babylon, follow, and then the harvest of the earth, Jesus' coming, is portrayed.

Chapters 15, 16–Just before this harvest but after the close of human probation the destiny of those receiving this mark is shown as seven plagues are described, which utterly defeat the forces of Babylon.

Chapter 17–Babylon's defeat is detailed, but... *(continued into next chapter)*

Chapter 18–God first warns His people in her ranks to leave before her destruction by the plagues.

Chapter 19–Christ's second coming follows, slaying His enemies and gathering up His friends.

Chapter 20–The earth is desolate for 1000 years, at the close of which Satan and sinners are destroyed.

Chapters 21, 22–The earth is made new and the New Jerusalem is established as the capital of the universe with God and Christ and His church as the ruling body.

Book of
REVELATION

REVELATION 1

1. The Revelation of Jesus Christ, which God gave unto him, to shew unto his servants things which must shortly come to pass; and he sent and signified it by his angel unto his servant John:

2. Who bare record of the word of God, and of the testimony of Jesus Christ, and of all things that he saw.

"In the Revelation all the books of the Bible meet and end," and in a special sense, it "is the complement of the book of Daniel" AA585. Much of what was sealed in the book of Daniel (Dan. 12:4) is unsealed in the book of Revelation, and the two must be studied together, 7BC724. In the book of Revelation Daniel is standing in his "lot at the end of the days," Dan. 12:13; 2SM109. Christ foresaw the warfare of Satan against the study of Revelation, and pronounced a blessing on all who read, hear, and obey the words of prophecy, GC342. "Which God gave." The chain of communication: God to Christ to His angel (Gabriel, DA99, 234) to John to God's servants.

3. Blessed is he that readeth, and they that hear the words of this prophecy, and keep those things which are written therein: for the time is at hand.

<u>*Blessed.*</u> *(Webster's Dictionary, "Giving happiness") This is the first of seven beatitudes of Revelation:*

1–Rev. 1:3, Blessed are those reading, hearing, keeping it.

2–Rev. 14:13, Blessed are the dead, dying in the Lord.

3–Rev. 16:15, Blessed is he that watches and keeps his garments.

4–Rev. 19:9, Blessed are those called to the Lamb's marriage supper.

5–Rev. 20:6, Blessed is the one having a part in the first resurrection.

6–Rev. 22:7, Blessed is he that keeps the sayings of this book.

7–Rev. 22:14, Blessed is the one obeying His commandments.

Those refusing to read, to hear, to do and practice the principles in this book will remain unblessed, GC341. The blessing is promised for God's people all through the centuries, PK548.

4. John to the seven churches which are in Asia: Grace be unto you, and peace, from him which is, and which was, and which is to come; and from the seven Spirits which are before his throne;

"In Asia" The literal churches located in the cities named had these characteristics, 3T201, 7BC957. But these churches and their characteristics were symbolic of the condition of the church at different periods of history, AA585.

"Which is, and which was, and which is to come." Christ declares that there was never a time when He was not in intimate companionship with God the Father, Ev615. From eternity Christ was in union with the eternal God, DA19, 1SM247. Original life, not borrowed, underived, is in Jesus, DA530. When the angel came to Christ's tomb and rolled back the stone, telling Him that the Father bade Him come forth, Christ came out by the power that was in the life within Himself, thus demonstrating the truth of His words in John 10:17,18: "I lay down My life that I might take it again...I have power to lay it down, and I have power to take it again," DA785. Only His humanity died, not His divinity, 1SM301.

"Seven spirits." "The seven-fold Holy Spirit." ANT. Grace and peace promised from Jesus and seven Spirits, Rev. 5:6; John 16:13.

5. And from Jesus Christ, who is the faithful witness, and the first begotten of the dead, and the prince of the kings of the earth. Unto him that loved us, and washed us from our sins in his own blood,

"First-begotten." Greek "first-born." *He was not the first to be raised from the dead in point of time, but He was the first in point of importance, the others having achieved this experience by virtue of His victory over death and the grave, 7BC21.*

6. And hath made us kings and priests unto God and his Father; to him be glory and dominion for ever and ever. Amen.

7. Behold, he cometh with clouds; and every eye shall see him, and they also which pierced him: and all kindreds of the earth shall wail because of him. Even so, Amen.

"They also which pierced Him." Raised to see Jesus come by a special resurrection will be those who took part in His crucifixion, as well as outstanding persecutors of God's people throughout the ages, and all who have died in the hope of His second coming since 1844, GC637.

8. I am Alpha and Omega, the beginning and the ending, saith the Lord, which is, and which was, and which is to come, the Almighty.

Christ is the Alpha and Omega, EV485. "The Almighty"—another name for Christ, as is "the Everlasting Father" in Isa. 9:6. If what the Bible says about Christ's deity is rejected, it is useless to argue with the rejectors since no reasoning, however logical, could persuade them, GC524.

9. I John, who also am your brother, and companion in tribulation, and in the kingdom with patience of Jesus Christ, was in the isle that is called Patmos, for the word of God, and for the testimony of Jesus Christ.

10. I was in the Spirit on the Lord's day, and heard behind me a great voice, as of a trumpet,

"The Lord's day" "The Sabbath... My holy day," Isa. 58:13, Jesus appeared to John on the seventh-day Sabbath, AA581. The Lord's day is the Sabbath, the seventh day, 6T12.

11. Saying, I am Alpha and Omega, the first and the last: and, What thou seest, write in a book, and send it unto the seven churches which are in Asia; unto Ephesus, and unto Smyrna, and unto Pergamos, and unto Thyatira, and unto Sardis, and unto Philadelphia, and unto Laodicea.

"The seven churches." Literally and symbolically. See vs. 4.

12. And I turned to see the voice that spake with me. And being turned, I saw seven golden candlesticks;

13. And in the midst of the seven candlesticks one like unto the Son of man, clothed with a garment down to the foot, and girt about the paps with a golden girdle.

"The Son of man." "Who looked like a man," TEV. Before He came to earth, Christ was taller than the angels, but at the start of His ministry He was slightly taller than the average-sized man, 4SG115. But now He is taller than Adam was, GC644, who was more than twice as tall as the average man of today, SR21.

14. His head and his hairs were white like wool, as white as snow; and his eyes were as a flame of fire;

"White like wool." the very whitest.

"Eyes were as a flame of fire." The most piercing.

15. And his feet like unto fine brass, as if they burned in a furnace; and his voice as the sound of many waters.

"His feet like unto fine brass." The shiniest.

"His voice as... many waters." Most resonant and strong.

16. And he had in his right hand seven stars: and out of his mouth went a sharp twoedged sword: and his countenance was as the sun shineth in his strength.

"Twoedged sword," the Word of God, Heb. 4:12,13.

17. And when I saw him, I fell at his feet as dead. And he laid his right hand upon me, saying unto me, Fear not; I am the first and the last;

18. I am he that liveth, and was dead; and, behold, I am alive for evermore, Amen; and have the keys of hell and of death.

"Amen," Heb. meaning "truly, we can be sure that I am alive for evermore."

19. Write the things which thou hast seen, and the things which are, and the things which shall be hereafter;

20. The mystery of the seven stars which thou sawest in my right hand, and the seven golden candlesticks. The seven stars are the angels of the seven churches: and the seven candlesticks which thou sawest are the seven churches.

"The seven stars." God's ministers, GW13, 14, AA371.

"Seven churches." Named in chapters 2 and 3 because they typified the condition of the church as a whole throughout the Chrstian era at various times, 7BC737.

REVELATION 2

1. Unto the angel of the church of Ephesus write; These things saith he that holdeth the seven stars in his right hand, who walketh in the midst of the seven golden candlesticks;

"Church of Ephesus." Approximately covers the time of the apostles. The seven churches outline the history of God's church to the close of time, AA583.

"He that holdeth... who walketh," signifies His constant care and attention to His church, AA58.

2. I know thy works, and thy labour, and thy patience, and how thou canst not bear them which are evil: and thou hast tried them which say they are apostles, and are not, and hast found them liars:

3. And hast borne, and hast patience, and for my name's sake hast laboured, and hast not fainted.

4. Nevertheless I have somewhat against thee, because thou hast left thy first love.

"Left thy first love." They had lost that which should have been everything to them, 7BC956.

5. Remember therefore from whence thou art fallen, and repent, and do the first works; or else I will come unto thee quickly, and will remove thy candlestick out of his place, except thou repent.

"And repent." Constant repentance is needed in order to have constant victory, 7BC959. And since repentance is defined as looking away from ourselves to Christ, this may and should be done constantly, MB131.

6. But this thou hast, that thou hatest the deeds of the Nicolaitans, which I also hate.

"Nicolaitans." *They taught, as some do today, that merely believing in Christ releases one from obeying the Ten Commandments, but Jesus strongly censured such a doctrine, 7BC957.*

7. He that hath an ear, let him hear what the Spirit saith unto the churches; To him that overcometh will I give to eat of the tree of life, which is in the midst of the paradise of God.

"Him that overcometh." *To be an overcomer it is necessary to be alert moment by moment, resisting evil on one hand, but trusting Christ constantly on the other, stayed by His power, SD368.*

8. And unto the angel of the church in Smyrna write; These things saith the first and the last, which was dead, and is alive;

"Smyrna." *The time of severe pagan persecution, around 100–313 A.D.*

9. I know thy works, and tribulation, and poverty, (but thou art rich) and I know the blasphemy of them which say they are Jews, and are not, but are the synagogue of Satan.

"Thy tribulation." *Persecutions, started by Nero about the time of Paul's martyrdom, were carried on with differing degrees of intensity for hundreds of years, GC40.*

"Synagogue of Satan." *Those under Satan's control who sin deliberately and work to make of no effect the Ten Commandments, 7BC958.*

10. Fear none of those things which thou shalt suffer: behold, the devil shall cast some of you into prison, that ye may be tried; and ye shall have tribulation ten days: be thou faithful unto death, and I will give thee a crown of life.

"Ten days." *The Emporor Diocletian persecuted severely, 303–313 A.D.*

"A crown of life." *Christ bestows each crown personally, RH, Nov. 22, 1898. These crowns are golden rings of light, 2SM260.*

11. He that hath an ear, let him hear what the Spirit saith unto the churches; He that overcometh shall not be hurt of the second death.

12. And to the angel of the church in Pergamos write; These things said he which hath the sharp sword with two edges;

"Pergamos." From Constantine's professed conversion, 323 A.D., to the establishment of the papacy, 538 A.D.

13. I know thy works, and where thou dwellest, even where Satan's seat is: and thou holdest fast my name, and hast not denied my faith, even in those days wherein Antipas was my faithful martyr, who was slain among you, where Satan dwelleth.

"Satan's seat." "When Cyrus captured the city of Babylon, the ancient seat of Satan's counterfeit of religion, the supreme pontiff of the Chaldean mysteries and his retinue of priests fled from the city and ultimately made their residence in Pergamos. Here they re-established their Babylon worship and made the king of Pergamos the chief pontiff of their religion. When Allatus III, the last of their priest-kings, died in 133 B.C., he bequeathed both his royal and priestly offices to Rome as Pontifex Maximus of the religion of the empire." Taylor G. Bunch, The Seven Epistles of Christ, p. 150.

14. But I have a few things against thee, because thou hast there them that hold the doctrine of Balaam, who taught Balac to cast a stumblingblock before the children of Israel, to eat things sacrificed unto idols, and to commit fornication.

"To eat things sacrificed unto idols, and to commit fornication." Two things forbidden by the Jerusalem council, Acts 15:29.

"To commit fornication." A church-state union, as took place during Constantine's time and beyond, when the church left her Master, Christ, and sought the support of the state, was considered spiritual adultery by God, James 4:4.

15. So hast thou also them that hold the doctrine of the Nicolaitans, which thing I hate.

"Nicolaitans." See Rev. 2:6.

16. Repent; or else I will come unto thee quickly, and will fight against them with the sword of my mouth.

17. He that hath an ear, let him hear what the Spirit saith unto the churches; To him that overcometh will I give to eat of the hidden manna, and will give him a white stone, and in the stone a new name written, which no man knoweth saving he that receiveth it.

"The hidden manna." The Holy Spirit, DA386. Concentrated Bible study with the Holy Spirit's aid gives new manna, and the Spirit also makes it effective, 6T163.

18. And unto the angel of the church in Thyatira write; These things saith the Son of God, who hath his eyes like unto a flame of fire, and his feet are like fine brass;

"Thyatira." The 1260-year period of papal supremacy, 538–1798, at which time the papacy received a mortal wound, Rev. 13:3,12.

19. I know thy works, and charity, and service, and faith, and thy patience, and thy works; and the last to be more than the first.

20. Notwithstanding I have a few things against thee, because thou sufferest that woman Jezebel, which calleth herself a prophetess, to teach and to seduce my servants to commit fornication, and to eat things sacrificed unto idols.

"To commit fornication," Rev. 2:14.

21. And I gave her space to repent of her fornication; and she repented not.

22. Behold, I will cast her into a bed, and them that commit adultery with her into great tribulation, except they repent of their deeds.

23. And I will kill her children with death; and all the churches shall know that I am he which searcheth the reins and hearts: and I will give unto every one of you according to your works.

"The reins." Heb., kidneys or loins. The ancients considered the kidneys the seat of human emotions, Ps. 33:11; Jer. 23:20; Dan. 2:30. The character is composed of these two ingredients, the thoughts and the emotions, 5T310.

24. But unto you I say, and unto the rest in Thyatira, as many as have not this doctrine, and which have not known the depths of Satan, as they speak; I will put upon you none other burden.

25. But that which ye have already hold fast till I come.

26. And he that overcometh, and keepeth my works unto the end, to him will I give power over the nations:

27. And he shall rule them with a rod of iron; as the vessels of a potter shall they be broken to shivers: even as I received of my Father.

28. And I will give him the morning star.

"The morning star." Christ, Rev. 22:16.

29. He that hath an ear, let him hear what the Spirit saith unto the churches.

REVELATION 3

1. And unto the angel of the church in Sardis write; These things saith he that hath the seven Spirits of God, and the seven stars; I know thy works, that thou hast a name that thou livest, and art dead.

"Sardis." In literal Sardis many of the members of the church had been converted by means of the ministry of the apostles, but they needed reproof because some had become indifferent, 7BC958. So was spiritual Sardis, the church of the Reformation, which may take its starting date from 1798, the end of the period of papal supremacy; or 1517, when Luther nailed his ninety-five propositions for debate to the church door at Wittenberg; or 1520, when Luther burned publicly the pope's order to retract or be excommunicated. As Reformation churches are yet in existence today, there is no terminal date.

"A name that thou livest and art dead." Wycliffe, 1320–1384, "the morning star of the Reformation," taught the two primary doctrines of Protestantism: salvation only through Christ, and the supreme authority of the Bible, GC89. And Luther's declaration, the principal thesis of Protestantism, was "The Bible and the Bible only as the rule of faith and doctrine." However, Protestants have drifted from this loyalty to the Bible, GC309, 310.

2. Be watchful, and strengthen the things which remain, that are ready to die: for I have not found thy works perfect before God.

3. Remember therefore how thou hast received and heard, and hold fast, and repent. If therefore thou shalt not watch, I will come on thee as a thief, and thou shalt not know what hour I will come upon thee.

"I will come on thee as a thief." Jesus here admonishes His people that the investigative judgment is taking place in the heavenly sanctuary and that it will soon pass to the cases of the living, GC490. This will take place when a national Sunday law is passed, 6T130; 7BC976.

4. Thou hast a few names even in Sardis which have not defiled their garments; and they shall walk with me in white: for they are worthy.

"A few names." The words of this verse apply only to those who become one with Christ. RH, Aug. 20, 1903. *"Their garments."* Robes of character, 7BC959.

5. He that overcometh, the same shall be clothed in white raiment; and I will not blot out his name out of the book of life, but I will confess his name before my Father, and before his angels.

"Book of life." Records the names of all who have entered God's service, GC480, and their good deeds, EW52. However, having one's name recorded in a church book does not necessarily mean it will also be written in the Lamb's book of life, 5T278, 4BC1166. In the investigative judgment, which began October 22, 1844, names recorded in the books of heaven, beginning with those who were the first dwellers on earth, are checked, closing with the living. Those with unrepented, unforgiven sins on their records will have their names removed, GC483.

6. He that hath an ear, let him hear what the Spirit saith unto the churches.

7. And to the angel of the church in Philadelphia write; These things saith he that is holy, he that is true, he that hath the key of David, he that openeth, and no man shutteth, and shutteth and no man openeth;

"Philadelphia." Applies to those who sincerely accepted the message of Christ's second coming to earth, which was proclaimed world-wide during the 1830s, symbolized by the first angel, Rev. 14:6,7, and all those since who accept the same

message and whose lives are so representative of Christ that there is not one word of condemnation in the message to this group. Only one other church, Smyrna, kept pure by severe persecution, shares this distinction, Rev. 2:8–11. That Philadelphia did not end in 1844 but continues through the seven last plagues is evident in at least two instances: (1) "He that openeth," Rev. 3:7. God opened this door before Philadelphia in 1844, EW41. (2) "I will also keep thee from the hour of temptation," Rev. 3:10. The latter rain, a special outpouring of the Holy Spirit to ripen earth's harvest and prepare the true people of God for Christ's coming, AA54, 55, also prepares them for the "hour of temptation," which they will meet during the seven last plagues, EW277. In 1888 it was written that the "hour of temptation" was yet to come to try every dweller upon earth, GC560–561. "Because you have kept My order to be patient, I will also keep you safe from the time of trouble which is coming upon the whole world, to test all the people on earth." Rev. 3:10, TEV.

8. I know thy works: behold, I have set before thee an open door, and no man can shut it; for thou hast a little strength, and hast kept my word, and hast not denied my name.

9. Behold, I will make them of the synagogue of Satan, which say they are Jews, and are not, but do lie; behold, I will make them to come and worship before thy feet, and to know that I have loved thee.

10. Because thou hast kept the word of my patience, I also will keep thee from the hour of temptation, which shall come upon all the world, to try them that dwell upon the earth.

11. Behold, I come quickly: hold that fast which thou hast, that no man take thy crown.

12. Him that overcometh will I make a pillar in the temple of my God, and he shall go no more out: and I will write upon him the name of my God, and the name of the city of my God, which is new Jerusalem, which cometh down out of heaven from my God: and I will write upon him my new name.

13. He that hath an ear, let him hear what the Spirit saith unto the churches.

14. And unto the angel of the church of the Laodiceans write; These things saith the Amen, the faithful and true witness, the beginning of the creation of God;

"Laodiceans." As early as 1852 Christians who profess to believe in Jesus' soon coming were told that their spiritual condition was described clearly by the portrayal of the Laodicean church, EW107, 108. They are warned that a continuation of a lukewarm condition will cause them to be vomited (Gr.) out of God's mouth, 1T485. Laodiceans will oppose the loud cry of the latter rain period, RH, Dec. 23, 1890. The message to the Laodiceans applies to all Christians who have not lived up to their profession and who will be rejected unless they repent, 2SM66. Those who have great professions but who are lukewarm and without zeal are described by this message to Laodicea, 4T87. But this message is for all Christians and must go to all churches, 6T77.

"The faithful and true witness." The Holy Spirit, the representative of Christ, not only utters truth, but is the truth, "the faithful and true witness," CT68.

"The beginning of the creation of God." The Greek word, "arche," here rendered "beginning," has both an active and a passive sense, and since Christ was not a created being (John 1:1–3,10,14), the correct translation of this word should be "beginner," or "the prime source of all God's creation" (NEB), or "the origin of all that God has created" (TEV).

15. I know thy works, that thou art neither cold nor hot: I would thou wert cold or hot.

16. So then because thou art lukewarm, and neither cold nor hot, I will spue thee out of my mouth.

"Spue." Gr. "emeo," vomit, suggesting the English word "emetic," a substance to induce vomiting. Laodiceans will be spued out, RH, Sept. 3, 1889.

17. Because thou sayest, I am rich, and increased with goods, and have need of nothing; and knowest not that thou art wretched, and miserable, and poor, and blind, and naked:

"Knowest not." God's people are deceived in regard to their true condition and yet honest in their ignorance, 3T253, and spiritually proud, DA300.

18. I counsel thee to buy of me gold tried in the fire, that thou mayest be rich; and white raiment, that thou mayest be clothed, and that the shame of thy nakedness do not appear; and anoint thine eyes with eyesalve, that thou mayest see.

"Buy of Me." From Christ one buys a life of willing obedience in exchange for a life of rebellion, 4T88.

"Gold." Faith and love, 2T36, 4T88, DA280; faith working through love, COL188; character, CM62; wisdom which is unto salvation, FE170.

"Tried in the fire." A faith that has been tested and purified by affliction and hardship.

"White raiment." Purity of character, Christ's righteousness imparted, 5T233, 4T88.

"Eyesalve." Eyesalve enables the receiver to discern sin in all its disguises, 4T88; to recognize the needs one has, CT42; to tell the difference between truth and error, ML73; to discern and escape Satan's traps, 5T233. It is also called God's Word, RH, Nov. 23, 1891; and the grace of God, 3T254, 7BC965.

19. As many as I love, I rebuke and chasten: be zealous therefore, and repent.

20. Behold, I stand at the door, and knock: if any man hear my voice, and open the door, I will come in to him, and will sup with him, and he with me.

"And will sup." Supper is provided by the one owning the door that is opened. What could feed this Guest, the Ruler of all creation, who owns everything? He thirsts for our

acknowledgement of His presence; He hungers for our under-standing and regard, DA191.

21. To him that overcometh will I grant to sit with me in my throne, even as I also overcame, and am set down with my Father in his throne.

"Am set down with My Father." As a priest Christ describes His work in this way, GC416.

22. He that hath an ear, let him hear what the Spirit saith unto the churches.

REVELATION 4

1. After this I looked, and, behold, a door was opened in heaven: and the first voice which I heard was as it were of a trumpet talking with me; which said, Come up hither, and I will shew thee things which must be hereafter.

"A door was opened in heaven." This door was opened between the holy and the most holy place of the heavenly sanctuary on October 22, 1844, when Christ, having finished His work in the holy place, passed into the most holy and took His stand before the ark of the testament, EW42.

"I will shew thee things which must be hereafter." The opening of the seven seals after 1844.

2. And immediately I was in the spirit; and, behold, a throne was set in heaven, and one sat on the throne.

"A throne was set." The investigative judgment, Dan. 7:9,10.

"One sat on the throne." God the Father presides at the investigative judgment while angels serve as witnesses and helpers, GC479.

3. And he that sat was to look upon like a jasper and a sardine stone: and there was a rainbow round about the throne, in sight like unto an emerald.

"A rainbow." The rainbow assures us of God's truthfulness and invariableness, COL148. As the rainbow is composed of sunshine and rain, so this rainbow signifies the combination of His justice and His mercy, Ed115. The rainbow declares that God's power is available for His people as they contend with sin as long as His throne is in existence, DA483.

4. And round about the throne were four and twenty seats: and upon the seats I saw four and twenty elders sitting,

clothed in white raiment; and they had on their heads crowns of gold.

"Four and twenty elders." These and the four living creatures represent the multitude that was resurrected when Christ arose (see Eph. 4:8 and Matt. 27:52,53) and who are now assisting Him in the heavenly sanctuary. They were workers for God who had been martyred, DA786, of every age from the days of creation to the time of Christ, EW184.

5. And out of the throne proceeded lightnings and thunderings and voices: and there were seven lamps of fire burning before the throne, which are the seven Spirits of God.

6. And before the throne there was a sea of glass like unto crystal: and in the midst of the throne, and round about the throne, were four beasts full of eyes before and behind.

7. And the first beast was like a lion, and the second beast like a calf, and the third beast had a face as a man, and the fourth beast was like a flying eagle.

"Four beasts." Gr. "living creatures." Commentators have suggested that the lion represents Christ's kingship, the calf or ox His service, the man as the humanity He assumed, and the flying eagle as His deity, comparing the way the four gospels present Jesus: with Matthew emphasizing Christ as a king, Mark as a servant, Luke as a human being, and John His divinity. Ezekiel 1:10 presents similar representations as "living creatures."

8. And the four beasts had each of them six wings about him; and they were full of eyes within: and they rest not day and night, saying, Holy, holy, holy, Lord God Almighty, which was, and is, and is to come.

9. And when those beasts give glory and honour and thanks to him that sat on the throne, who liveth for ever and ever,

10. The four and twenty elders fall down before him that sat on the throne, and worship him that liveth for ever and ever, and cast their crowns before the throne, saying,

11. Thou art worthy, O Lord, to receive glory and honour and power: for thou hast created all things, and for thy pleasure they are and were created.

REVELATION 5

(Of great significance to those living in these times, this chapter should be carefully studied because many are confused, 9T267.)

1. And I saw in the right hand of him that sat on the throne a book written within and on the backside, sealed with seven seals.

"A book." The only cases that come into review during the investigative judgment that began in 1844 are the avowed followers of God, GC480, and since the Book of Life records their names, this is the book to be opened at the judgment, GC483. The decisions made by the professed people of God are therein recorded, as was the determination of the leaders of the Jews at the time of Christ's trial; and their decision will appear before them in the book unsealed by Jesus, COL294.

2. And I saw a strong angel proclaiming with a loud voice, Who is worthy to open the book, and to loose the seals thereof?

3. And no man in heaven, nor in earth, neither under the earth, was able to open the book, neither to look thereon.

"No man." Gr. *"oudeis,"* *"not one,"* including all living beings in the universe with man.

4. And I wept much, because no man was found worthy to open and to read the book, neither to look thereon.

5. And one of the elders saith unto me, Weep not: behold, the Lion of the tribe of Judah, the Root of David, hath prevailed to open the book, and to loose the seven seals thereof.

6. And I beheld, and, lo, in the midst of the throne and of the four beasts, and in the midst of the elders, stood a Lamb as it

had been slain, having seven horns and seven eyes, which are the seven Spirits of God sent forth into all the earth.

"The lion...a lamb." To the ones refusing His invitation to salvation, Christ will eventually seem as a lion, while to His faithful followers He will be the Lamb of God, 6T404, AA589.

"As it had been slain." Thus Jesus is offering up His blood in the heavenly sanctuary because of His continually sinning people, 1SM344. When His followers live like Christ "who did no sin," I Peter 2:22, by His power being "perfect in Christ," Col. 1:28, and His likeness of character is reproduced in Christians, He can leave the sanctuary, exchanging His priestly robes for kingly, and return to earth, CT324, COL69.

"Seven horns." Seven is a number indicating perfection, while horns represent strength and glory: Deut. 33:17; Job 16:15; Psalm 75:4; Jer. 48:25; Amos 6:13; 7BC772.

"Seven eyes." Perfect wisdom and intelligence, the Holy Spirit, 7BC772.

"Spirits of God." Christ is presented everywhere by means of the Holy Spirit, Ed132. By the Spirit He is readily available to everyone, DA669.

7. And he came and took the book out of the right hand of him that sat upon the throne.

8. And when he had taken the book, the four beasts and four and twenty elders fell down before the Lamb, having every one of them harps and golden vials full of odours, which are the prayers of saints.

"Vials full of odours." This incense, Christ's intercessory perfection and righteousness, which ascends with the prayers of spiritual Israel, makes their service satisfactory to God, PP353. Christ's merit is the incense, 7BC970. Because human beings are corrupt and sinful, their prayers are not acceptable to God, but Christ places them in the censer with His righteousness and blood and offers them to the Father, and this incense is accepted

and the prayers, praise and confessions are heard, 1SM344, COL156.

9. And they sung a new song, saying, Thou art worthy to take the book, and to open the seals thereof: for thou wast slain, and hast redeemed us to God by thy blood out of every kindred, and tongue, and people, and nation;

"A new song." The cross of Christ will be the science and the song of the saved throughout eternity, GC651.

10. And hast made us unto our God kings and priests: and we shall reign on the earth.

"Kings and priests." The saved will reign as kings and priests, EW290, 291.

11. And I beheld, and I heard the voice of many angels round about the throne and the beasts and the elders: and the number of them was ten thousand times ten thousand, and thousands of thousands;

12. Saying with a loud voice, Worthy is the Lamb that was slain to receive power, and riches, and wisdom, and strength, and honour, and glory, and blessing.

"Saying." This hymn to the Lamb was proclaimed when Christ ascended to heaven, DA834, 835. It will be sung by the saints at the establishing of the New Earth, AA601, 602; GC671. And it will be sung by the redeemed and angels in eternity, 8T44.

13. And every creature which is in heaven, and on the earth, and under the earth, and such as are in the sea, and all that are in them, heard I saying, Blessing, and honour, and glory, and power, be unto him that sitteth upon the throne, and unto the Lamb for ever and ever.

14. And the four beasts said, Amen. And the four and twenty elders fell down and worshipped him that liveth for ever and ever.

REVELATION 6

1. And I saw when the Lamb opened one of the seals, and I heard, as it were the noise of thunder, one of the four beasts saying, Come and see.

"Opened one of the seals." *The deceased righteous are the first to have their cases examined in the investigative judgment, 1SM125. And only faithful church members, those professing to be God's people, are judged now; the unrighteous are judged during the thousand-year period or millennium, GC480.*

2. And I saw, and behold a white horse: and he that sat on him had a bow; and a crown was given unto him: and he went forth conquering, and to conquer.

"A white horse." *White symbolizes purity and freedom from sin. Isa. 1:18. A horse in prophecy is a symbol of a church, Hab. 3:8; Zech. 10:3.*

"He that sat on him." *Christ guides His true church, John 14:6, by means of His Holy Spirit, John 16:13.*

"A bow." *Christ's righteousness, Zech. 10:4; Gen. 49:24.*

"A crown." *Gr. "stephanos," a garland or wreath won in the Greek athletic contests, a fitting tribute to Christ who was victorious in His contest with the hosts of Satan in heaven and on earth. His followers, as Paul, will also be crowned with a crown of righteousness, 2 Tim. 4:8. So the white horse with Christ as its guide represents the righteous dead church members.*

3. And when he had opened the second seal, I heard the second beast say, Come and see.

4. And there went out another horse that was red: and power was given to him that sat thereon to take peace from the

earth, and that they should kill one another: and there was given unto him a great sword.

"Horse that was red." Red is a symbol of sin, Isa. 1:18. This horse represents the wicked dead church members, the first one of whom was Cain, who killed his brother after a church service, Gen. 4:3–8.

"Him that sat thereon." Satan, guide of the wicked, the red dragon, Rev. 12:3,9.

"To take peace from the earth." He wars against God's people, Rev. 12:17.

"A great sword." The power of the state, Rom. 13:4.

5. And when he had opened the third seal, I heard the third beast say, Come and see. And I beheld, and lo a black horse; and he that sat on him had a pair of balances in his hand.

"A black horse." Living righteous church members are judged after the cases of all the dead church members have been examined, 1SM125. Black represents mourning, mental distress, Jer. 14:2; 8:21; Joel 2:6; Nahum 2:10; Mal. 3:14, mg.; symbolizing the concern of the living righteous as they pass through the time of Jacob's trouble, Jer. 30:5–7; GC616–630; EW36, 37, 283, 284; PP202, 203.

"He that sat on him." God the Father, the Ancient of days, presides in the investigative judgment, Dan. 7:9,10; GC479.

"A pair of balances." Character is weighed in the balances of the sanctuary, CM51, 3T370, TM439. The church is weighed in the balances of the sanctuary, 5T83. Moral worth is also weighed there, RH, June 18, 1889, as is missionary work, 6T230. Belshazzar's character was "found wanting" by these balances, Daniel 5:27.

6. And I heard a voice in the midst of the four beasts say, A measure of wheat for a penny, and three measures of barley for a penny; and see thou hurt not the oil and the wine.

"A measure." A quart; a day's ration for a laboring man.

"A penny." A Roman denarius, a day's wage. "A quart of wheat for a whole day's wages, and three quarts of barley for a whole day's wages." TEV. Even among God's people there are differences in quality, some being more talented, more gifted, and more consecrated than others; but all are loved by God and cared for tenderly, and offered salvation–the penny that the laborers received in the parable of Matthew 20, which is Christ's character, RH, July 10, 1894. "The oil and the wine," represents the "little ones," those who resemble children in their understanding of Christ and the Bible, DA358, and the warning here is not to treat them indifferently or with scorn or in any way in which they may become discouraged or offended, 5T614.

7. And when he had opened the fourth seal, I heard the voice of the fourth beast say, Come and see.

8. And I looked, and behold a pale horse: and his name that sat on him was Death, and Hell followed with him. And power was given unto them over the fourth part of the earth, to kill with sword, and with hunger, and with death, and with the beasts of the earth.

"A pale horse." "Sickly pale," NEB. "Livid," Moffatt. The group of living wicked church members who plot against God's true people are here represented, with Death, the first death, as its rider; and Hell, the second death, accompanying, which is their eventual reward, Rom. 6:23; MS 13, 1895.

"The fourth part of the earth." Protestants, spiritualists, and Rome unite in a three-fold union to crush the fourth, God's remnant people, GC588.

9. And when he had opened the fifth seal, I saw under the altar the souls of them that were slain for the word of God, and for the testimony which they held:

"The fifth seal." Why should martyrs be judged in a class by themselves when they also are "righteous dead"? God gives them special honor, as He also does in giving them a distinctive dress in the New Earth, a border of red on their garments, EW18,

19. After the fifth seal is opened, the loud cry, described in Revelation 18 is given to call God's true followers out of Babylon in order that they "receive not of her plagues," 7BC968.

10. And they cried with a loud voice, saying, How long, O Lord, holy and true, dost thou not judge and avenge our blood on them that dwell on the earth?

11. And white robes were given unto every one of them; and it was said unto them, that they should rest yet for a little season, until their fellowservants also and their brethren, that should be killed as they were, should be fulfilled.

12. And I beheld when he had opened the sixth seal, and, lo, there was a great earthquake; and the sun became black as sackcloth of hair, and the moon became as blood;

13. And the stars of heaven fell unto the earth, even as a fig tree casteth her untimely figs, when she is shaken of a mighty wind.

"The sixth seal." This seal acts in a dual capacity; first, the great earthquake, the darkening of the sun and moon, and the falling of the stars were signs of Jesus' second coming, Matt. 24:29,30; Mark 13:25,27; Luke 21:25. Second, they are events that take place at the actual coming, Isa. 13:9,10; Joel 2:10,31; 3:13–15; GC641, 642.

14. And the heaven departed as a scroll when it is rolled together; and every mountain and island were moved out of their places.

15. And the kings of the earth, and the great men, and the rich men, and the chief captains, and the mighty men, and every bondman, and every free man, hid themselves in the dens and in the rocks of the mountains;

16. And said to the mountains and rocks, Fall on us, and hide us from the face of him that sitteth on the throne, and from the wrath of the Lamb:

17. For the great day of his wrath is come; and who shall be able to stand?

"Who shall be able to stand?" That question is answered by *the following chapter, 7:1–8, presenting the 144,000, those who will "be able to stand."*

REVELATION 7

1. And after these things I saw four angels standing on the four corners of the earth, holding the four winds of the earth, that the wind should not blow on the earth, nor on the sea, nor on any tree.

"Holding the four winds." Winds symbolize war, Jer. 25:32,33 and 49:36,37. When angels loose the winds after the world has been warned of its coming destruction, there will take place a time of carnage impossible to describe, Ed180. The entire world will be subjected to a period of strife worse than what took place at the destruction of Jerusalem, GC614. The four winds will be held by the four angels until Jesus completes His ministration in the sanctuary, and then the seven last plagues will fall, EW36. The winds also include elements of nature, storms, earthquakes, as well as agitation among nations, and these are kept in check by angels, TM444. But Christ will complete the sealing of His faithful ones, and then God will tell the restraining angels to allow Satan to have his way and destroy all those in his power, 7BC781.

2. And I saw another angel ascending from the east, having the seal of the living God: and he cried with a loud voice to the four angels, to whom it was given to hurt the earth and the sea,

3. Saying, Hurt not the earth, neither the sea, nor the trees, till we have sealed the servants of our God in their foreheads.

"Till we have sealed." The sealing is a progressive work, 1SM111. The living righteous will be sealed before probation's close, 1SM66. The latter rain falls upon a sealed people, 5T214. Only Sabbath keepers will be sealed, 7BC970. Some over ninety years of age who were living in 1889 were already sealed,

7BC982. The seal is not visible but is a firm grounding in the teaching of the Bible so that the receiver will stand firm and will not waver, 4BC1161. All receiving the seal are perfect in Christ, ready for heaven, 5T216, like Christ in nature, FILB287, completely reflecting His character, EW71. God's people must be tested on their allegiance to God and His Sabbath before they are sealed, 7BC976. The sealing of the 144,000 will take place during the closing work of the church, 3T266. Those who have died in the faith will be sealed in their graves, 2SM266, Psalm 17:15.

4. And I heard the number of them which were sealed: and there were sealed an hundred and forty and four thousand of all the tribes of the children of Israel.

"An hundred and forty and four thousand." This special group, Christ's honor guard (Rev. 14:4), have eight marks of identity:

1–They will be victorious over the beast, his image, and his mark, and since the mark is yet future, GC449, it is evident that this group has not as yet come into being.

2–They will be translated without seeing death.

3–They will go through the time of trouble, the seven last plagues.

4–They will take part in the time of Jacob's trouble.

5–They will stand without an intercessor through the final judgments.

6–They will be guileless and faultless.

7–They will see the earth subjected to famine and plague, specifically the fourth plague, the scorching heat of the sun.

8–They will be subjected to suffering from hunger and thirst, GC648, 649.

5. Of the tribe of Juda were sealed twelve thousand. Of the tribe of Reuben were sealed twelve thousand. Of the tribe of Gad were sealed twelve thousand.

6. Of the tribe of Aser were sealed twelve thousand. Of the tribe of Nepthalim were sealed twelve thousand. Of the tribe of Manasses were sealed twelve thousand.

7. Of the tribe of Simeon were sealed twelve thousand. Of the tribe of Levi were sealed twelve thousand. Of the tribe of Issachar were sealed twelve thousand.

8. Of the tribe of Zabulon were sealed twelve thousand. Of the tribe of Joseph were sealed twelve thousand. Of the tribe of Benjamin were sealed twelve thousand.

9. After this I beheld, and, lo, a great multitude, which no man could number, of all nations, and kindreds, and people, and tongues, stood before the throne, and before the Lamb, clothed with white robes, and palms in their hands:

"A great multitude." All the redeemed of all the ages make up this group, 1T78. "White robes and palms." The white robes signify Christ's righteousness and the palms represent victory, 7BC970. The multitude of the redeemed will be a happy, united family whose clothing will be thankfulness and glorification of God, which is the robe of Jesus' righteousness, MH506.

10. And cried with a loud voice, saying, Salvation to our God which sitteth upon the throne, and unto the Lamb.

11. And all the angels stood round about the throne, and about the elders and the four beasts, and fell before the throne on their faces, and worshipped God.

12. Saying, Amen: Blessing, and glory, and wisdom, and thanksgiving, and honour, and power, and might, be unto our God for ever and ever. Amen.

13. And one of the elders answered, saying unto me, What are these which are arrayed in white robes? and whence came they?

"Answered." "Asked me," TEV. "White robes." God's children are to wash their robes in Jesus' blood, 3T324.

14. And I said unto him, Sir, thou knowest. And he said to me, These are they which came out of great tribulation, and have washed their robes, and made them white in the blood of the Lamb.

"Great tribulation." Every one saved in heaven will have reached there through great tribulation, 5BC1097. "Made them white." The Holy Spirit is the soul's spiritual breath, imparting the very life of Christ, permeating the one receiving Him with the characteristics and qualities of Christ, DA805.

15. Therefore are they before the throne of God, and serve him day and night in his temple: and he that sitteth on the throne shall dwell among them.

16. They shall hunger no more, neither thirst any more; neither shall the sun light on them, nor any heat.

"Hunger no more." During the time of trouble severe poverty will be abroad in the world, accompanied by war, terror, and hunger, and even God's people may suffer hunger at times, but they are to remember that while God may test their steadfastness and trust, He will never desert them in their hardships, Ev240, 241.

17. For the Lamb which is in the midst of the throne shall feed them, and shall lead them unto living fountains of waters: and God shall wipe away all tears from their eyes.

"The Lamb." Jesus will lead His people along the River of Life while He explains to them how the hardships He permitted to come to them aided in perfecting their characters, 8T254.

REVELATION 8

1. And when he had opened the seventh seal, there was silence in heaven about the space of half an hour.

"The seventh seal...silence." The small black cloud, "the sign of the Son of man," Matthew 24:30, is seen coming from the east, and sitting upon it is Jesus, whose eyes as flames look at the people as He approaches, while the cloud becomes white and dazzling. The angels stop singing and there is some time of silence. But when Jesus says, "My grace is sufficient for thee," fear turns to joy, EW15, 16; 1T60; GC641.

"In heaven." The Bible speaks of three heavens: the first is the aerial, where birds fly, Rev. 19:17; the second is the stellar, Psalm 8:3; the third is where God's throne is, paradise, II Cor. 12:2–4; Rev. 2:7; 22:2,3. The silence takes place in the first or aerial heaven as Jesus approaches earth at His second coming.

"About the space of half an hour." Since prophetic time ended in 1844 (see 2SM108, 7BC971, 6BC1052), all time mentioned in prophecies since that time is literal, and this half hour must seem agonizingly long to His people as they search their hearts.

2. And I saw the seven angels which stood before God; and to them were given seven trumpets.

"Seven trumpets." From the seventh seal of the previous verse, opened as Jesus approaches the earth at His second coming, there is a flashback in order to fill in the details of the "little time of trouble" that transpires just before the plagues are poured out while the latter rain of the Holy Spirit is falling and the closing work of salvation is being accomplished, and the great time of trouble, the falling of the seven last plagues, EW85, 86. A trumpet in prophecy is a warning, Joel 2:1, and these warn

God's people of the "day of the Lord," the time of trouble, Isa.
27:13; Ex. 19:16; Isa. 58:1; Jer. 4:19,20; Zeph. 1:15,16.

"The Talmud [a collection of Jewish laws and commentary]
teaches that the blowing of trumpets signifies God's loud call to
repentance." F.C. Gilbert, Practical Lessons from the Experi-
ence of Israel for the Church of Today, page 520.

In Letter 109, 1890, Ellen White wrote that "trumpet after
trumpet is to be blown," showing that they were yet future in
1890, 7BC982.

3. And another angel came and stood at the altar, having a
golden censer; and there was given unto him much incense,
that he should offer it with the prayers of all saints upon the
golden altar which was before the throne.

"Another angel." Christ, our Intercessor, GC482–484.

"A golden censer." Jesus' merits, 1SM344, COL156.

"Much incense." The intercession of Christ's merits and
perfect righteousness, PP353, 7BC970.

"Prayers of all saints." Prayers have been ascending for the
descent of the Holy Spirit, and these have been treasured as they
have been accumulating. And now when the loud cry of the third
angel is sounding, the Holy Spirit is poured out abundantly in the
latter rain. Letter 96A, 1899.

4. And the smoke of the incense, which came with the prayers
of the saints, ascended up before God out of the angel's hand.

5. And the angel took the censer, and filled it with fire of the
altar, and cast it into the earth: and there were voices, and
thunderings, and lightnings, and an earthquake.

"Censer...filled...with fire of the altar, cast down into the
earth." This censer contains Christ's righteousness and the
prayers, praise and confessions of His people, 1SM344, COL
156. Fire from the altar represents the Holy Spirit, Acts 2:3,4;
AA39. When the contents of the censer are poured out upon the
earth, the latter rain begins, AA54, 55.

"Voices." The loud cry of the latter rain, EW271.

"Thunderings and lightnings." This represents the reaction of those rejecting the loud cry of the latter rain, GC607, 614, 615; EW56.

"An earthquake," The shaking follows the sealing, 4BC1161. There will be trials for God's people and also apostasies, but a purified church will unify, and the entire earth will be given the warning message, 6T400, 401.

6. And the seven angels which had the seven trumpets prepared themselves to sound.

7. The first angel sounded, and there followed hail and fire mingled with blood, and they were cast upon the earth: and the third part of trees was burnt up, and all green grass was burnt up.

"The first angel sounded." Just before the latter rain falls Satan will endeavor to counterfeit this outpouring of God's Spirit, GC464. Hail, frozen rain, his substitute for the warm, softening, shower of the latter rain; and fire, destructive, searing; is mingled with blood, representing guilt, Matt. 27:25. This trumpet, as well as those following, were yet in the future in 1890, when Ellen White wrote, "Trumpet after trumpet is to be sounded," 7BC982.

"Upon the earth." Territory of the United States, symbol of Protestantism, Rev. 13:11, GC440, which leads out in the counterfeit revival, 6T395.

"The third part of the trees." "Trees of righteousness," Isa. 61:3.

"All green grass." "All flesh is grass," Isa. 40:6. The message of Revelation 18 goes to true followers of Christ still in Babylon, "Come out of her, My people," vs. 4. As this message is heeded by His people, and they leave the fallen denominational churches, symbolized as Babylon, GC383, American Protestantism suffers a complete fall, and the United States leads the way in passing oppressive Sunday laws, which foreign nations follow,

6T395. Babylon, a three-fold union—Protestantism, Catholicism, Spiritualism (GC588, Rev. 16:13), has one of its members, Protestantism, "the third part," fallen or utterly devoid of the life-giving Spirit of God, "burnt up," GC389, 390.

8. And the second angel sounded, and as it were a great mountain burning with fire was cast into the sea: and the third part of the sea became blood.

"A great mountain." Babylon is called a "burnt mountain," Jer. 51:24,25. When Catholicism unites with spiritualism, GC588, Satan's counterfeit for the power of the Holy Spirit, GC464, it will be a burning mountain in the sea, the symbol for the Old World, Letter 109, 1890.

"Became blood." By rejecting the final message, Revelation 18, European Protestantism is also confirmed in guilt, Matt. 27:25.

9. And the third part of the creatures which were in the sea, and had life, died; and the third part of the ships were destroyed.

10. And the third angel sounded, and there fell a great star from heaven, burning as it were a lamp, and it fell upon the fountains of waters.

"A great star." As Christ warned (Matt. 24:5,24; Mark 13:6,21,22; Luke 21:8), false christs will appear, and finally Satan himself will impersonate Christ, GC624, in every particular, 5T696.

Roman Catholics expect Christ to return to this earth and assume kingship: "We can await the future with confidence, certain that the divine Providence will preserve the spiritual authority of Rome until the awful day when Christ Himself will take the place of His Vicar." Gilbert Bagnani, Rome and the Papacy, page 248, New York, Crowell.

Jews also expect a Messiah: "Says (Rabbi Louis) Finklestein: 'The great First Century Rabbi Eliezer once said: "The Messiah will never come until the Jewish people repent." When they asked him, "What if the Jews do not repent?" he answered: "The Lord will raise up a king worse than Haman to smite them, and then they will repent " This is just what happened. Hitler was something we never thought possible'." Time, "A Trumpet For All Israel," October 15, 1951.

God's faithful people will flee before infuriated mobs, doubt-less because they cannot accept this false christ, EW56.

"A lamp." "Then the third angel blew his trumpet and there fell from the sky a huge star, burning like a torch," Phillips. "A large star, burning like a torch, dropped from the sky and fell on a third of the rivers and on the springs of waters," TEV. Many occupying the pulpits of God's true church will have the torch of falsehood in their grasp, which they have lighted from Satan's, TM409, 410.

"The third part of the rivers and upon the fountains of waters." As the earth is a symbol for United States' Protestant-ism in the first trumpet, and the sea symbolizes European Protes-tantism in the second trumpet, so rivers and fountains of water that refresh the earth and replenish the sea represent the uncon-verted or natural man that provides membership or raw material for the churches. The unconverted or worldlings will join themselves to the great final ecumenical movement cemented by Spiritualism, GC588.

11. And the name of the star is called Wormwood: and the third part of the waters became wormwood; and many men died of the waters, because they were made bitter.

"Wormwood. A bitter and poisonous plant... Bible writers follow the oriental custom of symbolizing calamity, sorrow, and disappointment with plants of this nature," SDABD. Through Satan's bitter opposition to the loud cry of the latter rain many are led to reject the final warning and die spiritually.

12. And the fourth angel sounded, and the third part of the sun was smitten, and the third part of the moon, and the third part of the stars; so as the third part of them was darkened,

and the day shone not for a third part of it, and the night likewise.

"The fourth angel." As the first three trumpets included the whole wicked world, the fourth trumpet concerns the Remnant people not in Babylon, the church which is not Babylon, TM32–62. But this Remnant, subject to trials, delusions, and persecution from the forces of Babylon, will experience a shaking, which produces both a separation and a unification of her members, 6T400, 401; GC608.

"The sun was smitten, and the third part of the moon, and the third part of the stars." These heavenly bodies were symbols of the church in Jacob's time, Gen. 37:9,10, so the Remnant are hurt by persecution and a shaking.

"The day shone not." This marks the approach of the time when the gospel can no longer be proclaimed, as Jesus pointed out when He said, "I must work the works of Him that sent me, while it is day: the night cometh when no man can work," John 9:4. The day is the time for salvation, II Cor. 6:2, which ends in the night of the close of probation and the time of Jacob's trouble, when the righteous pray for deliverance from death as Jacob did. As Jacob wrestled until the break of day, so the righteous will agonize in prayer until the dawn of Jesus' coming.

13. And I beheld, and heard an angel flying through the midst of heaven, saying with a loud voice, Woe, woe, woe, to the inhabiters of the earth by reason of the other voices of the trumpet of the three angels, which are yet to sound!

"An angel flying." God sends important messages that He expects to be heeded when He represents them as being carried by an angel in flight, GC594. A message of exalted character, of purity, of power and of glory is to be accomplished by this representation, GC355. This message is world-wide and compelling, Ev476. So just before the close of human probation the angel of Revelation 18:1–3 and "another voice from heaven," verse 4, warn the true Christians to cut the ties that bind them to Babylon in order to escape the seven last plagues, GC603–612. When this

message, the last one that will be proclaimed, has been given and all of earth's inhabitants have declared their loyalty or disloyalty to God, an angel with a writer's inkhorn reports to Jesus in the most holy place, and He then proclaims that human probation is at an end; the seven last plagues are then begun, EW279–282, 52.

"Woe, woe, woe." A woe is pronounced in Rev. 12:12 for earth's inhabitants because the devil has come in wrath as he realizes he has but a short time left to work. A thrice-repeated woe would emphasize this danger during the time of trouble when the seven last plagues fall and his destructive and deceitful power would reach its climax, GC623.

REVELATION 9

1. And the fifth angel sounded, and I saw a star fall from heaven unto the earth: and to him was given the key of the bottomless pit.

2. And he opened the bottomless pit; and there arose a smoke out of the pit, as the smoke of a great furnace; and the sun and the air were darkened by reason of the smoke of the pit.

"A great furnace." The furnace is a symbol of God's presence, PP137. It is also a representation of the oppression of God's people, PP267, Deut. 4:20. The whole earth, as a furnace, is stoked by Satan to afflict the righteous, Isa. 48:10, and to attempt to blot them out, GC618; but God uses the furnace as a refiner to burn up the dross in the character of His people, I Cor. 3:13–15, that the character of Christ may be clearly seen, GC261.

"The sun and the air were darkened." The sun represents Christ, Mal. 4:2, MB64. Air symbolizes the Holy Spirit, John 3:8. These two heavenly Intercessors, Rom. 8:26, Heb. 7:25, are hidden from those on earth after the close of probation, Rev. 15:8.

3. And there came out of the smoke locusts upon the earth: and unto them was given power, as the scorpions of the earth have power.

"Locusts." Evil angels can exercise destructive power when permitted to do so by God, GC614. After the close of human probation the Spirit of God no longer puts forth His controlling power, and the people and their rulers are at the mercy of Satan and evil angels, 7T203, 204. Weapon-bearing men are led by evil angels to attempt to destroy God's people, GC635. Devils performing miracles will cause wonders to be seen in the sky, and

these demons will deceive kings and enlist them to join Satan in his final battle against God, GC624.

4. And it was commanded them that they should not hurt the grass of the earth, neither any green thing, neither any tree; but only those men which have not the seal of God in their foreheads.

"Should not hurt." The sealed righteous ones are divinely protected since their destruction would not at this time be "the seed of the church" as the blood of martyrs has in the past, but would only be a victory for Satan, GC634. Those with God's seal are shielded during the time of trouble, EW71. The Sabbath is the seal of God, GC640.

5. And to them it was given that they should not kill them, but that they should be tormented five months: and their torment was as the torment of a scorpion, when he striketh a man.

"Tormented." During the plagues the unfaithful ministers who have misled their parishioners will have to be subjected to more than just one or two of these plagues, EW124.

"Five months." Actual time, since all time references since the end of the 2300-day prophecy in 1844 are literal, 6BC1052, EW243, 2SM108, 7BC971. This could be the actual time it takes for the first four of the seven last plagues, Rev. 16:1–9. After listing the first four, GC628 says that these plagues are not world-wide or the dwellers on earth would be entirely destroyed.

6. And in those days shall men seek death, and shall not find it; and shall desire to die, and death shall flee from them.

7. And the shapes of the locusts were like unto horses prepared unto battle; and on their heads were as it were crowns like gold, and their faces were as the faces of men.

8. And they had hair as the hair of women, and their teeth were as the teeth of lions.

9. And they had breastplates, as it were breastplates of iron; and the sound of their wings was as the sound of chariots of many horses running to battle.

10. And they had tails like unto scorpions, and there were stings in their tails: and their power was to hurt men five months.

"Tails." Tails represent deceptions, Rev. 12:4, Isa. 9:15. Satan, the locusts' leader, is the chief deceiver, Rev. 12:9. He is ten times more skillful at deceit today than he was in the days of the apostles, GC277.

11. And they had a king over them, which is the angel of the bottomless pit, whose name in the Hebrew tongue is Abaddon, but in the Greek tongue hath his name Apollyon.

"Abaddon, Apollyon." "A destroyer," Satan would destroy all the birds if God didn't protect them especially, 8T273, DA341. At the crucifixion Satan had revealed himself as a destroyer, DA341. He desires to destroy everyone he possibly can, 7BC922.

12. One woe is past; and, behold, there come two woes more hereafter.

13. And the sixth angel sounded, and I heard a voice from the four horns of the golden altar which is before God,

"The sixth angel." As the fifth trumpet covered the period of the first four plagues, so the sixth trumpet sounds at the time of the fifth and sixth plagues, Rev. 16:10–16.

14. Saying to the sixth angel which had the trumpet, Loose the four angels which are bound in the great river Euphrates.

"Loose the four angels." A decree of death having been broadcast for the people of God, now sealed, Rev. 7:1–3, who will not yield to the majority and disregard the Sabbath, a spontaneous world-wide movement for their destruction begins. As the forces of evil move in upon their intended victims, a deep darkness settles down, plague five, stopping them in their tracks,

effectively "drying up" their onward march to the slaughter of God's people, plague six, GC635, 636.

15. And the four angels were loosed, which were prepared for an hour, and a day, and a month, and a year, for to slay the third part of men.

"An hour, and a day, and a month, and a year." This phrase has no significance as a measure of prophetic time, prophetic time having ended in 1844, EW243. "This very hour of this very day of this very month and year," TEV, and "this moment for this very year and month, day and hour," NEB. However, a prophecy based upon this phrase, made by Josiah Litch, a Millerite preacher, in 1840 concerning Turkey, aroused considerable interest and gave publicity to the preaching of the second advent, GC334, 335. The good that was accomplished in furthering the work of the Adventist preachers at that time suggests that God may have intended this to be a dual prophecy with Turkey as a secondary interpretation.

"To slay the third part of men." Humanity at this time may be divided into three parts:

1–The religious, composed of Christian denominations and heathen idol worshippers.

2–The irreligious, composed of atheists, agnostics, and infidels, whether communists or evolutionists.

3–The Remnant, God's sealed people. Under the leadership of Babylon, the world will be united to destroy "the third part," 7T182, GC635.

16. And the number of the army of the horsemen were two hundred thousand thousand: and I heard the number of them.

"Two hundred thousand thousand." "Two hundred million," TEV, NEB. A world-wide army of the future, organized for the sole purpose of destroying the people of God who are scattered in little companies throughout the world is here mentioned. "If this is a literal figure, it is no longer incredible in view of the

world population of 6,000,000,000 in the near future. In China alone in 1961 there were an 'estimated 200,000,000 armed and organized militiamen' (Associated Press Release, April 24, 1964.)" "Living Bible," page 1010.

17. And thus I saw the horses in the vision, and them that sat on them, having breastplates of fire, and of jacinth, and brimstone: and the heads of the horses were as the heads of lions; and out of their mouths issued fire and smoke and brimstone.

"Out of their mouths issued fire and smoke and brimstone." As the Two Witnesses, the Old and New Testaments, GC267, of Rev. 11:5, have fire proceeding from their mouths, showing that the word of God will condemn men who fail to heed it, so Babylon issues decrees backed by the power of the state with a death penalty attached. Although prevented from carrying out the death sentence against the Remnant, by the very act of condemnation they are considered just as guilty as if they had succeeded in effecting their desires, GC628.

18. By these three was the third part of men killed, by the fire, and by the smoke, and by the brimstone, which issued out of their mouths.

19. For their power is in their mouth, and in their tails: for their tails were like unto serpents, and had heads, and with them they do hurt.

20. And the rest of the men which were not killed by these plagues yet repented not of the works of their hands, that they should not worship devils, and idols of gold, and silver, and brass, and stone, and of wood: which neither can see, nor hear, nor walk:

"Repented not." The Holy Spirit's having been withdrawn at probation's close, repentance is impossible and earth's wicked inhabitants are under Satan's complete control, 7T203, 204. However, people will feel their need of a Guide, which they have continued to spurn until the time for repentance is past, and they

"will wander from sea to sea to seek the word of the Lord," Amos 8:11,12, but will be unsuccessful in their desperate search, GC629.

21. Neither repented they of their murders, nor of their sorceries, nor of their fornication, nor of their thefts.

REVELATION 10

1. And I saw another mighty angel come down from heaven, clothed with a cloud: and a rainbow was upon his head, and his face was as it were the sun, and his feet as pillars of fire:

"Mighty Angel." Jesus, 7BC971.

2. And he had in his hand a little book open: and he set his right foot upon the sea, and his left foot on the earth,

"A little book open." The book of Daniel, 2SM105. Daniel was opened; that is, was given special attention and study around 1830 and onward. Why are chapters 10 and 11 inserted here between the sixth and seventh trumpets? This flashback to 1830 is to show that a study of Daniel will strengthen one spiritually to pass through the time of trouble, TM115, PK547. Chapter 11, a description of the French Revolution, 1789–1799, is another flashback to show the need for a familiarity with the Bible truths in order to remain faithful, portraying the fearful results when a nation, France, rejected God and His Word.

"His right foot upon the sea, and his left foot upon the earth." The manner and place of standing shows that He has absolute authority over the world and also shows the work He is doing in the final movements of the struggle with the prince of evil, 7BC971.

3. And cried with a loud voice, as when a lion roareth: and when he had cried, seven thunders uttered their voices.

"Cried with a loud voice." The first angel's message, 1830 and onward to the present time, Rev. 14:6,7; GC311.

"Seven thunders." This was a description of things that would transpire during the proclamation of the first and second angels' messages; but as the faith of the people was to be tested, these

things were not to be revealed to them, 7BC971. The seven thunders also relate to events of the future which will be revealed, 7BC971, written 1900.

4. And when the seven thunders had uttered their voices, I was about the write: and I heard a voice from heaven saying unto me, Seal up those things which the seven thunders uttered, and write them not.

5. And the angel which I saw stand upon the sea and upon the earth lifted up his hand to heaven,

6. And sware by him that liveth for ever and ever, who created heaven, and the things that therein are, and the earth, and the things that therein are, and the sea, and the things which are therein, that there should be time no longer:

"There should be time no longer." After the close of the 2300-day prophecy in 1844, there would never again be a prophetic message involved with time, 6BC1052. In 1844 prophetic time came to an end, EW243. Prophetic periods ended when this announcement was made, 2SM108. The time that was to be "no longer" was prophetic time; after the period from 1842–1844 there can be no definite time prophecies, 7BC971. Beware of any time setters, TM55.

7. But in the days of the voice of the seventh angel, when he shall begin to sound, the mystery of God should be finished, as he hath declared to his servants the prophets.

"The seventh angel." That is, the seventh trumpet marks the taking over of earth under the rulership of Christ, Rev. 11:15, and is in substance the same as the seventh plague, Rev. 16:17.

8. And the voice which I heard from heaven spake unto me again, and said, Go and take the little book which is open in the hand of the angel which standeth upon the sea and upon the earth.

"The little book." Daniel, 2SM105.

9. And I went unto the angel, and said unto him, Give me the little book. And he said unto me, Take it, and eat it up; and it shall make thy belly bitter, but it shall be in thy mouth sweet as honey.

"Eat it up." *Truth understood and joyfully received is eating the book, 7BC971.*

"It shall make thy belly bitter." *"It was bitter to digest,"* *Moffatt.* *"It turned sour in my stomach,"* *TEV. When Christ did not appear in 1844, Millerite Adventists were bitterly disappointed.*

10. And I took the little book out of the angel's hand, and ate it up; and it was in my mouth sweet as honey: and as soon as I had eaten it, my belly was bitter.

11. And he said unto me, Thou must prophesy again before many peoples, and nations, and tongues, and kings.

"Thou must prophecy again." *After their disappointment some held fast and waited for further light, and as this came, they saw that as they had proclaimed the first and second angels' messages of Rev. 14:6–8, so it was their duty to give the third angel's message as well, Rev. 14:9–12, the final task of God's people before Jesus' return, GC432.*

REVELATION 11

1. And there was given me a reed like unto a rod: and the angel stood, saying, Rise, and measure the temple of God, and the altar, and them that worship therein.

"The Angel." The Lord Jesus commands John to measure both the temple and the worshippers, 7BC972. During the investigative judgment God is measuring the temple and the worshippers, 7T219.

2. But the court which is without the temple leave out, and measure it not; for it is given unto the Gentiles: and the holy city shall they tread under foot forty and two months.

"The court." The earth, 6T366.

"The holy city." The Church of Christ, oppressed by Rome, is here described, GC266. The holy city is God's true church, 4SP188.

"Forty and two months." The forty-two months and the 1260 days both reveal the time that the Roman power was to tyrannize Christ's Church. This period, beginning in 538, terminated in 1798 when an army of France imprisoned the ruling pope, who died in exile a year later, GC266.

3. And I will give power unto my two witnesses, and they shall prophesy a thousand two hundred and threescore days, clothed in sackcloth.

"My two witnesses." The Old and New Testaments, both of which testify for Christ and the plan of salvation, GC267.

"Clothed in sackcloth." When it was against the law to own and read the Bible, the Two Witnesses gave their messages in this manner, 4SP189. Such apparel indicates mourning, 2 Sam.

3:31; Jonah 3:6,8, because tradition had ascendancy over the Bible, GC269.

4. These are two olive trees, and the two candlesticks standing before the God of the earth.

"These are the two olive trees." They are described thus in Zech. 4:1–6; 1–14, perpetually furnishing oil for the lamps, whose light is also the Word of God, Psalm 119:105,130.

5. And if any man will hurt them, fire proceedeth out of their mouth, and devoureth their enemies: and if any man will hurt them, he must in this manner be killed.

6. These have power to shut heaven, that it rain not in the days of their prophecy: and have power over waters to turn them to blood, and to smite the earth with all plagues, as often as they will.

7. And when they shall have finished their testimony, the beast that ascendeth out of the bottomless pit shall make war against them, and shall overcome them, and kill them.

"Shall have finished." That is, "are finishing," GC268.

"The beast." Satan is in a different guise, 4SP192, GC268, 269. Satan ascends from the bottomless pit, as the earth is described during the thousand-year or millennium period, when he takes charge of the resurrected wicked, Rev. 20:7–9, GC663. The world has never seen such a violent war as that which was waged against God and His Word during the French Revolution, GC273.

"And kill them." The French National Assembly abolished the worship of God, and Bibles were gathered and scornfully destroyed.

8. And their dead bodies shall lie in the street of the great city, which spiritually is called Sodom and Egypt, where also our Lord was crucified.

"Sodom and Egypt, where also our Lord was crucified." Pharaoh's atheism and Sodom's immorality were demonstrated

in the French Revolution, GC269. And Jesus has declared that as His followers are treated, so are they dealing with Him personally, and will be recompensed similarly; therefore as His people were martyred, so He was being martyred, Matt. 25:31–46. The same teachings that produced the French Revolution are now being broadcast world-wide and they will involve the entire world in a similar conflict that convulsed France at that time, Ed229.

9. And they of the people and kindreds and tongues and nations shall see their dead bodies three days and an half, and shall not suffer their dead bodies to be put in graves.

"Three days and a half." On Nov. 26, 1793, a decree to abolish religion was issued in Paris. Three and a half years later the French government removed restrictions against the practice of religion, GC287.

10. And they that dwell upon the earth shall rejoice over them, and make merry, and shall send gifts one to another; because these two prophets tormented them that dwelt on the earth.

"Make merry." With jubilation men celebrated the reign of reason instead of God and His Word, GC274–276.

11. And after three days and an half the spirit of life from God entered into them, and they stood upon their feet; and great fear fell upon them which saw them.

12. And they heard a great voice form heaven saying unto them, Come up hither. And they ascended up to heaven in a cloud; and their enemies beheld them.

"They ascended." Since the French Revolution the Bible has been greatly honored with the organization of Bible societies to print and circulate the Word of God, which today is published in more than fifteen hundred languages and dialects, GC287.

13. And the same hour was there a great earthquake, and the tenth part of the city fell, and in the earthquake were slain of

men seven thousand: and the remnant were afrighted, and gave glory to the God of heaven.

"A great earthquake." France underwent a convulsion resembling an earthquake with the overturning of the home, the church, the state, and the social order of centuries, GC286.

"The tenth part of the city fell." France, one of the ten horns of the beast symbolizing Rome, Daniel 7:7,8, had been one of the most loyal "sons of the church" during the papal supremacy, but her becoming an atheistical government, and the one that under Napoleon's decree imprisoned the pope, giving that organization its "deadly wound," Rev. 13:3, caused "the city," Rome, to lose in the defection of France, a tenth of its support.

"Slain of men seven thousand." Titles of nobility were abolished and the French took the name Citizen.

14. The second woe is past; and, behold, the third woe cometh quickly.

15. And the seventh angel sounded; and there were great voices in heaven, saying, The kingdoms of this world are become the kingdoms of our Lord, and of his Christ; and he shall reign for ever and ever.

"The seventh angel." Christ takes the Kingdom at the sounding of the seventh trumpet, as He does at the pouring out of the seventh plague, Rev. 16:17, and the opening of the seventh seal, Rev.8:1, all of which are different descriptions of the same event.

16. And the four and twenty elders, which sat before God on their seats, fell upon their faces, and worshipped God,

17. Saying, We give thee thanks, O Lord God Almighty, which art, and wast, and art to come; because thou hast taken to thee thy great power, and hast reigned.

"Art to come." God comes with Christ at His second coming, AA590, Titus 2:13, I Thess. 4:16, "The Lord Himself" being God the Father and the "Archangel," Michael, being Christ.

18. And the nations were angry, and thy wrath is come, and the time of the dead, that they should be judged, and that thou shouldest give reward unto thy servants the prophets, and to the saints, and them that fear thy name, small and great; and shouldest destroy them which destroy the earth.

"And the nations were angry." This anger, the same *"fury"* that stirs up the king of the north in Daniel 11:44, is caused by the success and vigor of the final warning in the loud cry of the third angel, GC607, 614, 615; EW279.

"And thy wrath is come." The seven last plagues, Rev. 15:1.

"And the time of the dead, that they should be judged." The judgment of the wicked that takes place during the thousand years, those dead in sin, Daniel 7:22; Rev. 20:4; I Cor. 6:1–3; EW291; GC660, 661.

"And that Thou shouldst give reward unto thy servants." Eventually the righteous inherit the New Earth, Rev. 21:1–4, while the wicked, whose sin and rebellion has operated to *"destroy the earth,"* will be destroyed themselves, Rev. 20:9; Mal. 4:1. This anger of nations, the wrath of God, and the judgment time of the dead are definite and separate, one following another, EW36.

19. And the temple of God was opened in heaven, and there was seen in his temple the ark of his testament: and there were lightnings, and voices, and thunderings, and an earthquake, and great hail.

"And the temple of God was opened in heaven." This is both a flashback to October 22, 1844, when Christ passed from the holy to the most holy place in the heavenly sanctuary to begin the antitypical Day of Atonement, and His people were shown that the Ten Commandemnts, there sacredly enshrined, were still decidedly in force, including the command to honor the seventh-day Sabbath; and also a preview, when the temple in heaven will be opened and the stone tablets containing the commandments will be shown to all, 7BC972. This will be done

by a hand holding them in the sky with words so clear that all can read them, and takes place after the seventh plague, just before Christ's appearing at His second coming, GC639. It will again transpire after the thousand years at the coronation of Jesus, GC688.

"And there were lightnings, and voices, and thunderings, and an earthquake, and great hail." The seventh plague, Rev. 16:17–21. Since the fourth commandment was not a test until after the temple of God was opened in heaven, after 1844, 2T693, a view of one of the plagues, God's wrath, is presented as a warning not to refuse to honor the Sabbath and thereby receive the mark of the beast, which brings God's wrath, as the third angel shows, Rev. 14:9–11.

REVELATION 12

1. And there appeared a great wonder in heaven; a woman clothed with the sun, and the moon under her feet, and upon her head a crown of twelve stars:

"And there appeared." As the seven churches span the course of the history of Christ's Church from His earthly sojourn to the New Earth, and as the seven seals outline the events that transpire during the investigative judgment and its culmination in Christ's return and acceptance of those whose records are clear, so the seven trumpets warn God's people who live in the closing days of earth's history to be prepared for the fiery tests of the little time of trouble, which is followed by the great time of trouble when the seven last plagues are poured out without mixture of mercy. This preparation is obtained by "eating the little book," Daniel, of Revelation 10:9,10, strengthening the mind with the Word of God, GC593, and obeying implicitly the Two Witnesses, the Old and New Testaments, Revelation 11. Thus the subjects of Christ's Kingdom will be made ready. And now to show the course of history leading up to Christ's taking the rulership of earth, a flashback shows Satan's rebellion in Heaven, which took place before earth's creation, SR19,20; Jesus' birth; and the persecution of His followers, with finally an all-out war against the Remnant Church by Satan, the dragon. Details of that war, Satan's defeat, and the establishment of a new earth are spelled out in the rest of Revelation, chapters 13–22.

"A woman." A woman in prophecy symbolizes a church, Isa. 51:16; Jer. 6:2. Weak, imperfect, requiring constant warning and counseling, Christ's church is supremely beloved by Him, TM49. All the hosts of Heaven are concerned with the welfare of

God's people on earth, particularly esteemed by the Father, TM41.

"Clothed with the sun." Jesus, Malachi 4:2.

"Moon under her feet." The prophecies of the Old Testament that provide the foundation for the faith of the church, John 5:39; Luke 24:27,44–47.

"Twelve stars." The twelve apostles or angels, messengers (Rev. 1:20), which signify God's ministers, GW13, 14. The twelve patriarchs in the Old Testament represented Israel, so the twelve apostles represent the Christian church, AA19.

2. And she being with child cried, travailing in birth, and pained to be delivered.

"With child." Christ, Isa. 9:6, the Man-Child, vs. 5.

3. And there appeared another wonder in heaven; and behold a great red dragon, having seven heads and ten horns, and seven crowns upon his heads.

"A great dragon." Primarily, Satan, vs. 9; but secondarily, Rome, GC38; but also ruling powers that war against God's people, TM39.

"Having seven heads." Assyria, Egypt, Babylon, Medo-Persia, Greece, Rome, the United States. Why these nations and in this order? When the Hebrew people left Egypt, they were an independent nation, DA77. So whatever nation from that time removes the independence or attempts to bring Israel, literal or spiritual, into bondage, becomes one of Satan's persecuting heads. As to the order in which the heads appear, one authority writes: "It was Jeremiah's lot to witness the death of his country. Beginning his career as the tottering Assyrian empire relaxed its grip on its former holdings, in forty short years Jeremiah saw it fall victim to the imperial ambitions first of Egypt, then of Babylon, before finally watching it destroy itself in a futile attempt to get free of the latter." John Bright, The Anchor Bible, Jeremiah, p. xxviii. New York: Doubleday 1965. And since the papacy is, as Thomas Hobbes, the British historian, observes,

"the ghost of the deceased Roman Empire, crowned and seated upon the grave thereof," it would hardly be fitting to consider Rome in its pagan and papal phases as separate heads.

"Ten horns." Kingdoms, Dan. 8:8,22. Ten horns appear on the beasts of Revelation 13 and 17, and apparently are identical with the ten horns of the nondescript beast of Daniel 7, which symbolized Rome's division into the ten kingdoms of Europe.

"Seven crowns." Indicates a ruling office, so Satan in effect ruled through these earthly powers, John 12:31; 14:30; 16:11.

4. And his tail drew the third part of the stars of heaven, and did cast them to the earth: and the dragon stood before the woman which was ready to be delivered, for to devour her child as soon as it was born.

"His tail." Lies, deceptions, Isa. 9:15, PP38–42, GC496–498, John 8:44.

"The third part." Satan deceived one third of the angels, who were cast out of Heaven with him, vs. 9, 5T291, 3T115. In a secondary interpretation this can be applied to Rome that in its conquest of Judah removed its king, "one third" of its stars or ruling powers, the Sanhedrin and priests making up the two-thirds which remained.

"To devour," Attempted unsuccessfully by Herod, Matt. 3:13–16; accomplished by Pilate, Matt. 27:24–26, Satan operated through the Roman government.

5. And she brought forth a man child, who was to rule all nations with a rod of iron: and her child was caught up unto God, and to his throne.

6. And the woman fled into the wilderness, where she hath a place prepared of God, that they should feed her there a thousand two hundred and threescore days.

"A thousand two hundred and threescore days." The time of papal supremacy when God's people were oppressed by Rome, 538–1798, GC266.

7. And there was war in heaven: Michael and his angels fought against the dragon; and the dragon fought and his angels,

"War in heaven." Envious and then jealous because God had not consulted him as He had Christ concerning the creation of man, Lucifer eventually openly rebelled, becoming Satan, EW15, 3SG36.

8. And prevailed not; neither was their place found any more in heaven.

9. And the great dragon was cast out, that old serpent, called the Devil, and Satan, which deceiveth the whole world: he was cast out into the earth, and his angels were cast out with him.

"Deceiveth the whole world." Satan's ability now to deceive is ten times greater than it was in Christ's day, and it will continue to increase, 2SG277. God's people are in perilous times and they must receive constant counsel from Christ because Satan's temptations are becoming more and more powerful, CT322.

10. And I heard a loud voice saying in heaven, Now is come salvation, and strength, and the kingdom of our God, and the power of his Christ: for the accuser of our brethren is cast down, which accused them before our God day and night.

"The accuser." Gossip is used by Satan to sow discord and strife, 4T195, 607. Those who do this are Satan's helpers, GC519. Angels of God oversee the work of God and they will correct the leaders of the church when necessary without any need for assistance from critics, 1T204.

"Cast down." Satan revealed his true character as a liar and murderer when he engineered Christ's death, so from that time on he could not confuse the loyal angels as to his motives and purposes, DA761.

11. And they overcame him by the blood of the Lamb, and by the word of their testimony; and they loved not their lives unto the death.

"Unto the death." Because martyrdom puts the victom beyond the power to be hurt further or to be overcome, every martyr has died a conqueror, PP77.

12. Therefore rejoice, ye heavens, and ye that dwell in them. Woe to the inhabiters of the earth and of the sea! for the devil is come down unto you, having great wrath, because he knoweth that he hath but a short time.

"A short time." Satan's wrath increases as his time to work grows shorter, and his destructive and deceptive activities reach their climax during the time of trouble, GC623.

13. And when the dragon saw that he was cast unto the earth, he persecuted the woman which brought forth the man child.

14. And to the woman were given two wings of a great eagle, that she might fly into the wilderness, into her place, where she is nourished for a time, and times, and half a time, from the face of the serpent.

"Wings of a great eagle." "When God delivers His people from persecution and oppression, He represents it as bearing them on eagle's wings," Ex. 19:4.

"A time, and times, and half a time." "Three years and a half," NEB; "Three and a half years," TEV. See Rev. 12:6 and Dan. 7:25.

15. And the serpent cast out of his mouth water as a flood after the woman, that he might cause her to be carried away of the flood.

"As a flood." "Like a river," TEV. A river in prophecy symbolizes persecution or a persecuting kingdom, Isa. 8:7.

16. And the earth helped the woman, and the earth opened her mouth, and swallowed up the flood which the dragon cast out of his mouth.

"The earth helped the woman." *The Waldenses found refuge in the mountains, GC64; the Pilgrims found shelter in the Dutch Republic and then in the New World with others who valued religious freedom, GC290–296.*

17. And the dragon was wroth with the woman, and went to make war with the remnant of her seed, which keep the commandments of God, and have the testimony of Jesus Christ.

"Was wroth." *Frustrated at his unsuccessful attempts to crush the church in the wilderness, Satan will concentrate his efforts toward destroying the Remnant Church. Having gained control of the nominal churches, he will become enraged at a little group that continue their full allegiance to God, so he will influence governments to pass oppressive laws that violate God's law in an attempt to cause their destruction, 5T472, 473. The Sabbath will be declared illegal, RH, March 9, 1886. A law will command citizens to give honor to the first day of the week while disregarding the seventh day, 1T353, 354; GC39, 640. Pastors will encourage their followers to disobey God's law and will persecute those who keep it, GC655, 656.*

"Keep the commandments." *This is the principal characteristic of the Remnant, and it shows that this will be the main point at issue in the final struggle between the dragon and the church, GC445–450.*

"Testimony of Jesus Christ." *Rev. 19:10 defines this as "the spirit of prophecy," indicating that Jesus is guiding and directing, showing His presence, testifying to His Church by means of prophetic guidance, the other definite quality by which the Remnant Church may be recognized. Prophetic guidance was given in December, 1844, when Ellen Harmon, later Mrs. James White, was given her first vision. Her work, she explained, was to direct people back to a neglected Bible, the greater light, by means of her writings, which she termed a lesser light, CM125. The Bible provides knowledge superior to all other writings, she*

testified, urging all to read and study its pages for their mental and spiritual good, 5T686.

REVELATION 13

1. And I stood upon the sand of the sea, and saw a beast rise up out of the sea, having seven heads aned ten horns, and upon his horns ten crowns, and upon his heads the name of blasphemy.

"A beast." An earthly kingdom or nation, Dan. 7:25. The dragon, primarily Satan and secondarily Rome, handed over his "power, his seat," his capital, "and great authority" to the ecclesiastical kingdom of papal Rome: "Out of the ruins of political Rome arose the great moral Empire in the 'giant form' of the Roman Church," A. C. Flick, The Rise of the Medieval Church, 1900, page 150.

"Out of the sea" Europe is a restless sea of nationalities, populations, and languages, GC440.

"Seven heads." See Rev. 12:3.

"Ten horns." In Rev. 12:3 the heads are crowned, showing that Satan has operated behind the scenes during the rule of these various empires, but here the horns are crowned, indicating that this kingdom comes to power during the times of Rome in its divided state, among the separate nations of Europe, 538–1798.

"Blasphemy. The crime of assuming to oneself the rights and qualities of God," Barnhart's College Dictionary. In New Testament times this was so understood, for Christ was accused of blasphemy for forgiving a man his sins, Mark 2:5–7; Luke 5:20,21; and for claiming to be God, John 10:33,36. This power claims to be able to forgive sins: "St. Alphonsus de Liguori, writing under the imprimatur of papal authorities, says, 'The priest has the power of the keys, or the power of delivering sinners from hell, of making them worthy of paradise, and of

changing them from slaves of Satan into the children of God. And God Himself is obligated to abide by the judgment of His priests, and either not to pardon or to pardon.'" <u>Dignities</u> <u>and</u> <u>Duties</u> <u>of</u> <u>the</u> <u>Priest</u>, *edited by Eugene Grimm, 1927, page 27. It also claims "the qualities of God": "The Pope is of so great dignity and so exalted that he is not a mere man, but as it were God, and the vicar of God... The Pope is of so great authority and power that he can modify, explain, or interpret even divine laws." Translated from Lucius Ferraris, "Papa II,"* <u>Prompta</u> <u>Bibliotheca</u>, *Vol. VI, pages 25–29, cited in 4BC831.*

2. And the beast which I saw was like unto a leopard, and his feet were as the feet of a bear, and his mouth as the mouth of a lion: and the dragon gave him his power, and his seat, and great authority.

"And the beast which I saw was like..." See Daniel 7 for the nations represented by these various animals. This composite beast has borrowed the religions and characteristics of the countries represented, incorporating them into a religious system desired by the multitudes, GC567, who want a way to forget God that appears to be a way of remembering Him, GC572.

3. And I saw one of his heads as it were wounded to death; and his deadly wound was healed: and all the world wondered after the beast.

"Wounded to death." This took place in 1798 when the pope was taken captive by the army of France, GC439, 579.

"His deadly wound was healed." This transpires when "all that dwell on the earth shall worship him," vs. 8, except the faithful few of God's people, GC579.

One important event which aided this healing took place in 1929 when the Lateran Treaty restored temporal power to the pope by giving him the rule of Vatican City, a section of Rome about 108.7 acres in size.

"All the world wondered." "The whole earth was amazed,"
TEV.

4. And they worshipped the dragon which gave power unto the beast: and they worshipped the beast, saying, Who is like unto the beast? who is able to make war with him?

"They worshipped." Worship and serve are synonymous,
Matt. 4:10. Honoring the beast's and the dragon's day of
worship instead of God's to get or keep a job, or to go along with
the crowd equals worshipping that power, GC449, 450.   Times-2yr

5. And there was given unto him a mouth speaking great things and blasphemies; and power was given unto him to continue forty and two months. Time, times & half a time — 180 Daniel 7:25

"Forty and two months." The 1260 years of papal supremacy.

6. And he opened his mouth in blasphemy against God, to blaspheme his name, and his tabernacle, and them that dwell in heaven.

"Blaspheme his name and his tabernacle." By assuming
God's titles for his own and substituting "the sacrifice of the
mass" for the heavenly sanctuary service.

"That dwell in heaven." The prerogatives of Deity have been
claimed by this power, and powers and virtues have been
claimed for Mary that pertain only to Christ. Power is claimed
also over the angels of God: "Indeed, the excellence and power
of the Roman pontiff is not only in the sphere of heavenly things,
earthly things, and those of the lower regions, but even above the
angels, than whom he himself is greater." Translated from
Lucius Ferraris, Papa II, Prompta Bibliotheca, volume VI, page
27, cited in 7BC818.

7. And it was given unto him to make war with the saints, and to overcome them: and power was given him over all kindreds, and tongues, and nations.

8. And all that dwell upon the earth shall worship him, whose names are not written in the book of life of the Lamb slain from the foundation of the world.

"Shall worship him." Keeping the first day of the week deliberately instead of God's day means worshipping the beast or his image, TM133.

"The book of life." "All people living on earth will worship it, that is, everyone whose name has not been written, before the world began, in the book of the living that belongs to the Lamb that was slain," TEV. The book of life records the names of all who have entered God's service, having accepted Jesus, GC480, 483. It contains the good deeds of God's people, EW51. Not all the names recorded in church records are in the book of life, 5T278; RH, Feb. 10 and Apr. 19, 1891.

9. If any man have an ear, let him hear.

10. He that leadeth into captivity shall go into captivity: he that killeth with the sword must be killed with the sword. Here is the patience and the faith of the saints.

11. And I beheld another beast coming up out of the earth; and he had two horns like a lamb, and he spake as a dragon.

"Another beast." A lamb-horned beast, as well as a dragon and a leopard-bodied animal, represent governments that would disregard the law of God and afflict His people, 7BC972.

"Out of the earth." The Greek word for coming up is used for growing plants, "to spring up." "Like a silent seed we grew into empire," G. A. Townend, *The New World Compared with the Old,* page 462, cited in GC440. When the leopard-bodied beast was going "into captivity," verse 10, in 1798, the United States was becoming prominent and powerful, GC439–441.

"Two horns like a lamb." When this beast was arising in 1798, these horns showed youthfulness, innocency, and mildness, fitly representing the two foundation principles of civil and religious liberty, republicanism and Protestantism, GC441. It is when the majority demand, as is consistent with the democracy, a Sunday

law, and legislators yield to the demand, 5T451, PK605, that this power will speak "as a dragon." A horn in prophecy symbolizes a persecuting power, Zech. 1:18,19, and this is the paradoxical way in which a democratic principle will be used to persecute, to speak as the dragon, Satan.

12. And he exerciseth all the power of the first beast before him, and causeth the earth and them which dwell therein to worship the first beast, whose deadly wound was healed.

"Causeth the earth." When the United States joins the papacy in compelling the observance of Sunday and the disregard of the Sabbath, every nation on earth will fall into step with this program, 6T18, 395; GC579.

"To worship." Keeping the first day of the week equals worship of the beast, TM133. Jesus stated that serving a power equaled worshipping it, Matt. 4:10.

13. And he doeth great wonders, so that he maketh fire come down from heaven on the earth in the sight of men,

"Maketh fire come down." This will be accomplished by means of spiritualism, EW59. Satan will bring down fire from heaven, GC612. He will do it to try to prove to men that he is a god. Series B, Special Testimonies, Number 6, page 33.

14. And deceiveth them that dwell on the earth by the means of those miracles which he had power to do in the sight of the beast; saying to them that dwell on the earth, that they should make an image to the beast, which had the wound by a sword, and did live.

"Miracles." These are actual miracles, not impostures or pretense, GC553, SR395.

"Image to the beast." The United States will form this image to the beast, a union of church and state, 2SM380, when united Protestant churches shall coerce the government to compel observance of their laws and to support their organizations, 4SP278, GC445.

15. And he had power to give life unto the image of the beast, that the image of the beast should both speak, and cause that as many as would not worship the image of the beast should be killed.

"Should be killed." There will be a decree made that will require all to observe Sunday and disregard the seventh-day Sabbath under penalty of death, 1T353, 354. This decree will bring on the time of Jacob's trouble, causing people to agonize in prayer as Jacob did, EW36, 37. Those refusing to observe this decree, continuing to honor God's Sabbath, will be sealed, 5T216.

16. And he causeth all, both small and great, rich and poor, free and bond, to receive a mark in their right hand, or in their foreheads:

"A mark." It is only when Sunday observance is enforced by law, after the people of the world have been enlightened concerning God's requirement to honor the true Sabbath, that the one refusing to keep the seventh day receives the mark of the beast, GC449.

"Right hand or in their foreheads." Some will cooperate with the pro-Sunday/anti-Sabbath laws for the sake of employment or social pressure even when they know better; it's more "handy." Such receive the mark in the right hand. Others are convinced that their church or the state has a right to promote such legislation in spite of a plain statement to the contrary in the Bible, and such receive the mark of apostasy in the forehead.

17. And that no man might buy or sell, save he that had the mark, or the name of the beast, or the number of his name.

"No man might buy or sell." In the future it will be impossible for God's people to sell a thing, no matter what the price is, 5T152.

"The mark." This is not a mark that can be seen by men, 7BC980.

18. Here is wisdom, Let him that hath understanding count the number of the beast: for it is the number of a man; and his number is Six hundred threescore and six.

"The number of a man." The beast represents a mere human organization.

"Six hundred threescore and six." "The numerical value of the letter of his name will make up this number," reads a former Douay version footnote on this verse. The following question was asked and answered in the Roman Catholic paper, Our Sunday Visitor, April 18, 1915: "What are the letters supposed to be in the Pope's crown and what do they signify, if anything?" "The letters inscribed in the Pope's mitre are these" 'Vicarius Filii Dei,' which is Latin for Vicar of the Son of God. Catholics hold that the Church which is a visible society must have a visible head." Taking, as was suggested in the Douay footnote, "the numerical value" of the Roman numerals of this phrase

V=5
I=1
C=100
A=0
R=0
I=1
V=5
S=0

F=0
I=1
L=50
I=1
I=1

D=500
E=0
I=1

THE TOTAL IS: 666

REVELATION 14

1. And I looked, and, lo, a Lamb stood on the mount Sion, and with him an hundred forty and four thousand, having his Father's name written in their foreheads.

"Mount Zion." Heaven is where God's throne is, Psalm 48:2. Having met the test, having achieved victory over the beast, his image, and his mark, the one hundred and forty-four thousand are presented in their official role as the Lamb's honor guard, GC648, 649, to be with Him forever, verse, 4. See Rev. 7:1–8. The church's final work is the sealing of this group, 3T266.

"His Father's name." This represents the submission of the mind to an unreserved acceptance and following of God's orders, SD370.

2. And I heard a voice from heaven, as the voice of many waters, and as the voice of a great thunder: and I heard the voice of harpers harping with their harps:

3. And they sung as it were a new song before the throne, and before the four beasts, and the elders: and no man could learn that song but the hundred and forty and four thousand, which were redeemed from the earth.

4. These are they which were not defiled with women; for they are virgins. These are they which follow the Lamb whithersoever he goeth. These were redeemed from among men, being the firstfruits unto God and to the Lamb.

"Not defiled." Free from the influences of apostate ecumenical churches, "women" in prophecy, having faced death rather than compromise themselves, 5T53.

"They are virgins." "Chaste," NEB. "They are as pure as virgins," Williams, NT. In the parable Christ termed the ten

151

young bridesmaids virgins because they claimed a pure religious belief, COL406.

"Firstfruits." They are the first installment of the great harvest of the redeemed that will be resurrected, GC637, 644. Translated without dying, Hebrews 11:5, they are considered "the firstfruits unto God and to the Lamb," GC649.

5. And in their mouth was found no guile: for they are without fault before the throne of God.

"No guile." "No lie was found on their lips; they are fault-less," NEB. It is better to go hungry than tell a lie, 4T495.

"Without fault." Perfection means wholehearted keeping of the Ten Commandments, 1T416. At every stage of spiritual growth God's people may be perfect, but they must continue to grow, Ed106. There may be a daily growth in perfection, MH503. When God's people possess Christ's perfection of character, they will be sealed, 6BC1118. We should strive now to be perfect in Christ, GC623. No one can claim to be perfect in his flesh with its sinful tendencies, but he may be spiritually perfect in his soul, 2SM32. Christ requires perfect characters, possible only by becoming acquainted with the Bible, CT454. Jesus in His life on earth showed that human beings may be perfect by letting God direct their lives, AA531. He came to show man how by connecting himself with God and Christ he could keep every commandment, 1SM253.

6. And I saw another angel fly in the midst of heaven, having the everlasting gospel to preach unto them that dwell on the earth, and to every nation, and kindred, and tongue, and people,

"Another angel." The first angel gave a warning of the approach of the judgment, and this message was preached from about 1830–1844 by William Miller and his followers in the United States and by others in other countries, producing a world-wide movement. They were mistaken as to the event, interpreting the cleansing of the sanctuary as the purifying of the

earth by the fire of Jesus' coming, but not as to the time, October 22, 1844, when Christ passed from the holy place of the heavenly sanctuary to the most holy place to make a final investigation and cleansing of His people before returning to gather them to Himself, GC299–342 and 355–374.

7. Saying with a loud voice, Fear God, and give glory to him; for the hour of his judgment is come: and worship him that made heaven, and earth, and the sea, and the fountains of waters.

"A loud voice." The power provided by the Holy Spirit.

"And worship Him that made." The world was created by the Word of God, Psalm 33:6,9. It was not evolved over long ages of time, according to the doctrine of evolution, commonly believed and taught today, Ed128. So it is impossible to worship the God of Heaven unless we believe He is the Creator, Ed130. The first angel's message is a Sabbath message, reminding humans of their Creator, GC452. It calls all people to return to a belief in God as Creator, PP45. If the Sabbath had always been kept, idolaters or atheists would never have existed, PP336.

8. And there followed another angel, saying, Babylon is fallen, is fallen, that great city, because she made all nations drink of the wine of the wrath of her fornication.

"Another angel." These three angels symbolize a group of Christians who accept what the Bible teaches without the additions of tradition, and carry the good news of Jesus' soon coming to the inhabitants of earth, 7BC979.

"Babylon is fallen." This announcement applies to denominational organizations that have become corrupted even though they were originally pure, and as it comes after the first angel's judgment hour message, it shows that it is given in the last days, so it cannot apply to the Roman Catholic Church only, GC383. Protestant churches have become more and more corrupt since this announcement was first proclaimed in the summer of 1844, EW237–240, 273, 304; GC375–390. The complete fall of

Babylon is yet future, it being a continuing process at the present time, GC390. Babylon comes from the word "babel," confusion, and in the Bible represents various false or apostate religions, GC381.

"That great city." Greek, "association."

"She made all nations drink." She has not as yet made "all" nations drink her wine, but eventually she will, GC389, 390.

"Wine of the wrath of her fornication." When national leaders drink Babylon's wine of false doctrine, they become enraged at the Remnant that will not disregard God's Sabbath, TM62. This wine of false teaching includes a belief in the natural immortality of the soul, never-ending burning of the wicked, that Jesus is not a God who has existed eternally with the Father, and elevating Sunday above the true Sabbath, TM61.

9. And the third angel followed them, saying with a loud voice, If any man worship the beast and his image, and receive his mark in his forehead, or in his hand,

"The third angel followed." When Jesus on October 22, 1844, went from the holy place to the most holy place in the sanctuary in Heaven, He sent this angel to alert His Remnant people against the beast and its image and to warn them to cling to God and His teaching even at the cost of life itself, EW254. His people were shown the Sabbath truth, His seal, and the world was warned of the penalty for receiving the mark of apostasy, GC433–460.

"Worship the beast." By doing what this organization demands instead of what God requires, worship is rendered, the terms worship and serve being synonymous, Matt. 4:10. One does this by keeping the first day of the week and disregarding the seventh, TM133.

"His image." The "beast" is the papacy, and the image is a similar form of government that accepts the help of the State to enforce its laws and support its institutions, apostate Protestantism, GC445.

"His mark." When all have been given warning of the binding claims of the true Sabbath, and when Sunday-keeping is enforced by law, those turning away from the fourth commandment to accept the first day, either because it's handier or more convenient to cooperate with the State or because they conscientiously believe that the church authorities have the right to modify God's law, receive the mark in the hand or forehead, GC449. See Rev. 13:16. Those Christians who have compromised little by little with the customs of the world will easily be led to cooperate with the program of the image to save themselves from the threat of jail or death, 5T81. But one doesn't receive the mark by refraining from labor on Sunday and using the time to do missionary work, 9T23. The decree that will cause all to take a stand one way or the other is the requirement to honor Sunday while disregarding God's Sabbath, 1T353, 354. See Rev. 13:17.

10. The same shall drink of the wine of the wrath of God, which is poured out without mixture into the cup of his indignation; and he shall be tormented with fire and brimstone in the presence of the holy angels, and in the presence of the Lamb:

"Without mixture." In the punishment visited in the seven last plagues God's wrath is poured out with no mixture of mercy, an element that has always been present in previous judgments, GC629. Always before God has remembered mercy in His wrath, Hab. 3:2.

11. And the smoke of their torment ascendeth up for ever and ever: and they have no rest day nor night, who worship the beast and his image, and whosoever receiveth the mark of his name.

12. Here is the patience of the saints: here are they that keep the commandments of God, and the faith of Jesus.

"The patience of the saints." "This calls for endurance on the part of God's people, those who obey God's commandments and are faithful to Jesus," TEV. Endurance is needed because the people of God will be persecuted for honoring the Sabbath,

9T229. They will flee into the wilderness, yet many will be jailed and left to starve, GC626, 627. A great many will be martyred, Maranatha, page 199.

13. And I heard a voice from heaven saying unto me, Write, Blessed are the dead which die in the Lord from henceforth: Yea, saith the Spirit, that they may rest from their labours; and their works do follow them.

"Blessed are the dead." Those faithful ones who have watched and worked for Jesus' speedy return will be resurrected just before He comes at a special resurrection, GC637.

14. And I looked, and behold a white cloud, and upon the cloud one sat like unto the Son of man, having on his head a golden crown, and in his hand a sharp sickle.

15. And another angel came out of the temple, crying with a loud voice to him that sat on the cloud, Thrust in thy sickle, and reap: for the time is come for thee to reap; for the harvest of the earth is ripe.

"Another angel." This angel is an addition to the three that gave their messages earlier. This angel informs Jesus that the harvest of the righteous ones, the wheat, is to be gathered, GC644, 645.

16. And he that sat on the cloud thrust in his sickle on the earth; and the earth was reaped.

17. And another angel came out of the temple which is in heaven, he also having a sharp sickle.

"Another angel." The wicked are represented as grapes to be trodden in the winepress of the earth. The first harvest of the grapes is at Jesus' return when the wicked are slain by one another and by the glory of His coming, GC656, 657. The second harvest is "without the city," verse 20, one thousand years later when the fire of God descends, GC672, 673; EW294.

18. And another angel came out from the altar, which had power over fire; and cried with a loud cry to him that had the

sharp sickle, saying, Thrust in thy sharp sickle, and gather the clusters of the vine of the earth; for her grapes are fully ripe.

19. And the angel thrust in his sickle into the earth, and gathered the vine of the earth, and cast it into the great winepress of the wrath of God.

20. And the winepress was trodden without the city, and blood came out of the winepress, even unto the horse bridles, by the space of a thousand and six hundred furlongs.

"A thousand and six hundred furlongs." "Two hundred miles long and about five feet deep," TEV.

REVELATION 15

1. And I saw another sign in heaven, great and marvellous, seven angels having the seven last plagues; for in them is filled up the wrath of God.

"The seven last plagues." It was seen that when Jesus' work in the heavenly sanctuary was completed, the four angels would free the four winds they were holding (see Rev. 7:1), and then the seven last plagues will fall, EW36. At that time God will tell the angels to permit Satan to bring his destructive efforts as he chooses upon the wicked, their days of probation having ended, 7BC781. Natural forces and wars are the "winds" that are held, TM444. There will be fearsome conflict and struggle, Ed180.

"The wrath of God." This is a separation *"from the presence of the Lord,"* II Thessalonians 1:9. It was thus that the wrath of God fell upon His Son at the crucifixion, causing Christ such agony that His physical pain was scarcely felt, DA753, and it was this sense of separation from God that broke His heart with sorrow, GC540.

2. And I saw as it were a sea of glass mingled with fire: and them that had gotten the victory over the beast, and over his image, and over his mark, and over the number of his name, stand on the sea of glass, having the harps of God.

"They that had gotten the victory." These are the one hundred forty and four thousand who have lived through the seven last plagues and have been translated without seeing death at Jesus' coming, GC648.

3. And they sing the song of Moses the servant of God, and the song of the Lamb, saying, Great and marvellous are thy works, Lord God Almighty; just and true are thy ways, thou King of saints.

"The song of Moses." As Israel was delivered from earthly powers at the Red Sea under the leadership of Moses, so spiritual Israel will be delivered from earthly powers, the beast and his image, by Christ's intervention, GC635, 636.

"The song of the Lamb." This represents deliverance from sin, the one hundred forty and four thousand being *"without fault,"* Rev. 14:5.

4. Who shall not fear thee, O Lord, and glorify thy name? for thou only art holy: for all nations shall come and worship before thee; for thy judgments are made manifest.

5. And after that I looked, and, behold, the temple of the tabernacle of the testimony in heaven was opened:

6. And the seven angels came out of the temple, having the seven plagues, clothed in pure and white linen, and having their breasts girded with golden girdles.

"Seven plagues." Calamity often appears greater before it comes than when it actually occurs, but that is not the case with these plagues; it is impossible to imagine or describe the severity of the experience, GC622.

7. And one of the four beasts gave unto the seven angels seven golden vials full of the wrath of God, who liveth for ever and ever.

8. And the temple was filled with smoke from the glory of God, and from his power; and no man was able to enter into the temple, till the seven plagues of the seven angels were fulfilled.

REVELATION 16

1. And I heard a great voice out of the temple saying to the seven angels, Go your ways, and pour out the vials of the wrath of God upon the earth.

Why does God permit the plagues to occur?

Five reasons are suggested:

1–Plagues one to four show men that they have been fighting God, but they curse Him instead of repenting.

2–The hardships produced help to perfect the saints.

3–The wicked are caught in the very act of a death decree.

4–Before the universe the saints demonstrate that they would rather die than sin.

5–Also before the whole universe it is demonstrated what conditions would be like if Satan had full control.

The first four plagues are not world-wide, GC628. But plagues five, six and seven are, GC635–637. Satan's deceitfulness and destructiveness will achieve their highest points during this time, GC623. Looking for a scapegoat to blame, the wicked persuade themselves that if they can rid the earth of God's people, the plagues will stop, so they publish a decree of annihilation, and then the saints are plunged into the agonizing "time of Jacob's trouble," EW36, 37. The people of God, scattered in remote areas and imprisoned, are fed by angels, but their enemies go hungry and thirsty, EW282.

2. And the first went, and poured out his vial upon the earth; and there fell a noisome and grievous sore upon the men which had the mark of the beast, and upon them which worshipped his image.

"Upon the earth." Territory of the United States, Rev. 13:11, GC440, 628.

3. And the second angel poured out his vial upon the sea; and it became as the blood of a dead man: and every living soul died in the sea.

"Upon the sea." The old world, Europe, is termed a "turbulent sea" of people, GC440.

4. And the third angel poured out his vial upon the rivers and fountains of waters; and they became blood.

"The rivers and fountains of waters." As waters represent people, Rev. 17:15, and as the population branched out from the Middle East after the Flood, Gen. 8:4, this could represent the southwestern Asiatic territory.

5. And I heard the angel of the waters say, Thou art righteous, O Lord, which art, and wast, and shalt be, because thou hast judged thus.

6. For they have shed the blood of saints and prophets, and thou hast given them blood to drink; for they are worthy.

"They have shed." The hosts of the wicked by their death decree are as guilty of the death of the saints as if they had slain them by their own hands, GC628. Because every one on earth has made his choice for good or evil and probation time has ended, the martyrdom of God's people at this time would not be a witness to convert anyone and would be a triumph for Satan; therefore God will allow none of his faithful ones to be killed, GC634.

7. And I heard another out of the altar say, Even so, Lord God Almighty, true and righeous are thy judgments.

8. And the fourth angel poured out his vial upon the sun; and power was given unto him to scorch men with fire.

"The sun." The Far East is noted for sun worshippers. The Japanese flag, for example, bears the symbol of the rising sun, so this territory will be plagued by its god, the sun.

9. And men were scorched with great heat, and blasphemed the name of God, which hath power over these plagues: and they repented not to give him glory.

10. And the fifth angel poured out his vial upon the seat of the beast; and his kingdom was full of darkness; and they gnawed their tongues for pain,

"The seat of the beast." Greek, "area, region." The people of the whole world will be united at this time under the leadership of the papacy, 7T182, so this plague is universal, an inky darkness blacker than night settles upon the earth, GC636, stopping the forces of evil in their tracks as they attempt to destroy God's people at the decreed hour, GC635, 636.

11. And blasphemed the God of heaven because of their pains and their sores, and repented not of their deeds.

12. And the sixth angel poured out his vial upon the great river Euphrates; and the water thereof was dried up, that the way of the kings of the east might be prepared.

"Euphrates." That the Euphrates represents a persecuting force can be demonstrated by syllogisms; that is, a reasoning in which two statements are made and a logical conclusion drawn from them. For example, a river in prophecy represents a persecuting force or kingdom, Isa. 8:7; the Euphrates is a river, Deut. 11:24; therefore the Euphrates is a persecuting force or kingdom. Or, a flood represents persecution, Rev. 12:13,15,16; the Euphrates is a flood, Joshua 24:2,3; therefore the Euphrates is persecution. This attempt to massacre is worldwide, GC635.

"Dried up." As the hosts of evil are rushing to destroy the saints, the inky blackness of the fifth plague, doubtless a darkness like that which fell upon Egypt, "even darkness which may be felt," Exodus 10:21, halts them abruptly, "drying up" their rush to slay, GC635, 636.

"The kings of the east." The kings, God, Christ, and the angels seem to come to this earth from the east because of the rotation of

the earth. They signal the persecuted ones to look up, GC636, EW285, 286.

13. And I saw three unclean spirits like frogs come out of the mouth of the dragon, and out of the mouth of the beast, and out of the mouth of the false prophet.

"Three unclean spirits." This flashback shows how demons working miracles will persuade earth's leaders that it is for their best interest not to tolerate the stubborn minority element that refuses to cooperate with the general program of Sunday exaltation, GC624.

"Like frogs," Frogs catch their prey with their tongues. An ecumenical force that cuts across denominational lines in what is considered a great religious revival is glossolalia, "talking in tongues." But this is a meaningless chatter, created by the speaker himself, assisted by Satan, 1T412, who attempts by this and by other means, such as so-called miraculous healings, to counterfeit the genuine revival and reformation which will be produced by the latter rain of the Holy Spirit, GC464.

That this speaking in tongues activity is a uniting force was suggested by R. J. McDonald, president of the spiritualists, in his address to the officers, trustees, and delegates of the Seventy-seventh Annual Spiritualistic Convention in 1964, who stated, "One of the newest phenomena in the field of religion is the interest in glossolalia, which has captured the interest of major Protestant sects... When Modern Spiritualism came into being in 1848, a great many early mediums experienced this phenomenon, and it has continued to some extent in our organization... No doubt glossolalia will be of great assistance to the merging groups."

"The false prophet." A comparison of Rev. 13:14 and 19:20 shows that this term represents the United States, the beast with lamb-like horns, GC439–442.

14. For they are the spirits of devils, working miracles, which go forth unto the kings of the earth and of the whole world, to gather them to the battle of that great day of God Almighty.

"The battle." This battle's outcome is pictured in Rev. 19:11–19. "The great battle is not between nation and nation, but between earth and heaven," James White, "Thoughts on the Great Battle," RH, Jan. 21, 1862.

15. Behold, I come as a thief. Blessed is he that watcheth, and keepeth his garments, lest he walk naked, and they see his shame.

"I come as a thief." This pertains to the "time" of coming, not the "manner" of coming, for His coming will be noisy, Psalm 50:3.

"Garments." "The garments of salvation...the robe of righteousness," Isa. 61:10; the "wedding garment," Matt. 22:11–13. Those who seem to have "the ornaments of the sanctuary" but don't wear the garment of His righteousness will at the time of the attempted enforcement of the Sunday law's death decree, be naked, unprotected, PK188.

16. And he gathered them together into a place called in the Hebrew tongue Armageddon.

"And he gathered." The correct translation is "they," not "he." "So they assembled the kings," NEB. "Then the spirits brought the kings," TEV.

"Armageddon." Heb. "mount of assembly, appointment, congregation." The Remnant, jailed, scattered, proscribed, hunted, and sentenced to death, are all over the world, and in their "time of Jacob's trouble," plead for God's help while the hosts of the wicked move up to destroy them in one night, GC635. The battle of Armageddon will be fought when Jesus leads Heaven's armies down to rescue His beleaguered people, 6T406.

17. And the seventh angel poured out his vial into the air, and there came a great voice out of the temple of heaven, from the throne, saying, It is done.

"The seventh angel," God's voice, saying, "It is done," is so powerful it causes an earthquake so great that the sea boils like a pot and islands disappear, GC636, 637.

18. And there were voices, and thunders, and lightnings; and there was a great earthquake, such as was not since men were upon the earth, so mighty an earthquake, and so great.

19. And the great city was divided into three parts, and the cities of the nations fell: and great Babylon came in remembrance before God, to give unto her the cup of the wine of the fierceness of his wrath.

20. And every island fled away, and the mountains were not found.

21. And there fell upon men a great hail out of heaven, every stone about the weight of a talent: and men blasphemed God because of the plague of the hail; for the plague thereof was exceeding great.

"Weight of a talent." "A hundred pounds," TEV.

REVELATION 17

1. And there came one of the seven angels which had the seven vials, and talked with me, saying unto me, Come hither; I will shew unto thee the judgment of the great whore that sitteth upon many waters:

"The great whore." Again using a syllogism, a form of reasoning in which two statements are made and a logical conclusion drawn from them, the identity of this woman can be determined: The woman of Revelation 17 is Babylon, verse 5. Babylon is the name applied to fallen denominational churches, TM61; therefore, this woman represents fallen denominational churches. In this chapter the eradication and final ruin of all religious organizations that have served and partaken of the ideas of the papacy is predicted, 7BC983. The condition of corrupt and apostate religions was shown to John in this prophecy, PP167. "Religion cannot sink lower than when it is somehow raised to a state religion. It then becomes an avowed mistress," Heine, 1822.

"Sitteth upon many waters." "Peoples, and multitudes, and nations, and tongues," verse 15.

2. With whom the kings of the earth have committed fornication, and the inhabitants of the earth have been made drunk with the wine of her fornication.

"Wine of her fornication." This is false doctrine:

(a) The immortality of the soul.

(b) The eternal punishment of the wicked.

(c) Christ was merely a good man and not a member of the Godhead, in existence with God from eternity.

(d) Teaching that the first day of the week is the Sabbath for Christians and showing contempt for the true Sabbath, TM61.

3. So he carried me away in the spirit into the wilderness: and I saw a woman sit upon a scarlet-coloured beast, full of names of blasphemy, having seven heads and ten horns.

"A scarlet-coloured beast." Satan, Rev. 12:3, with his identical "seven heads and ten horns," but lacking the crowns because he now operates through the apostate church, which rides upon him rather than kings as formerly.

4. And the woman was arrayed in purple and scarlet colour, and decked with golden and precious stones and pearls, having a golden cup in her hand full of abominations and filthiness of her fornication:

5. And upon her forehead was a name written, MYSTERY, BABYLON THE GREAT, THE MOTHER OF HARLOTS AND ABOMINATIONS OF THE EARTH.

"Mystery." "A name with a secret meaning," NEB. "A name that has a secret meaning," TEV.

"Babylon." Different types of counterfeit and apostate religions, GC381. Many different sects, GC383, yet united under the headship of the papacy, held together by Satan, 7T182.

6. And I saw the woman drunken with the blood of the saints, and with the blood of the martyrs of Jesus: and when I saw her, I wondered with great admiration.

7. And the angel said unto me, Wherefore didst thou marvel? I will tell thee the mystery of the woman, and of the beast that carrieth her, which hath the seven heads and ten horns.

8. The beast that thou sawest was, and is not; and shall ascend out of the bottomless pit, and go into perdition: and they that dwell on the earth shall wonder, whose names were not written in the book of life from the foundation of the world, when they behold the beast that was, and is not, and yet is.

"Was and is not." "The beast you saw (once) was, but (now) is no more...and he is (yet) to come," Amplified Bible. Satan openly led one third of the angels when he rebelled in Heaven, Rev. 12:7, PP41, GC497. After leading Adam and Eve into sin by means of the serpent, he has gone underground, operating through kings and kingdoms and apostate churches to carry out his purposes, his "is not" stage, GC438. After the thousand years he will openly lead the multitude of the wicked against the New Jerusalem, telling his deluded followers that he is the rightful ruler of the city, GC663.

"Bottomless pit.": The earth during the thousand years, GC658.

"Perdition." When devoured by the flame, GC672, 673.

9. And here is the mind which hath wisdom. The seven heads are seven mountains, on which the woman sitteth.

"The seven heads are seven mountains." A mountain in prophecy represents a kingdom or nation, Jer. 51:25; Dan. 2:35,44.

10. And there are seven kings: five are fallen, and one is, and the other is not yet come; and when he cometh, he must continue a short space.

"Five are fallen." When Israel left Egypt, it became an independent nation, DA77. So whatever nation from that time on removes the independence of God's chosen ones becomes a "head" of Satan, from Assyria, number one, to the United States, number seven. At the time John received his vision, five had "fallen," and the "one is" was Rome, whose Emperor Domitian had exiled him to Patmos. For the identity of the first three we are indebted to The Anchor Bible, Jeremiah, John Bright, page xxviii, "It was Jeremiah's lot to witness the death of his country. Beginning his career as the tottering Assyrian empire relaxed its grip on its former holdings, in forty short years Jeremiah saw it fall victim to the imperial ambitions first of Egypt, then of Babylon, before finally watching it destroy itself in a futile

attempt to get free of the latter." Following Babylon, the fourth head was Medo-Persia, which in turn was conquered by Greece, the fifth, Dan. 8:20,21.

"The other is not yet come." American territory was to remain unknown to the then civilized world for another one thousand four hundred years.

"Continue a short space." The "short space" could be a comparison with Rome's entire existence of over five hundred years or merely a reference to when the seventh head will be causing "the earth and its inhabitants" to "worship the first beast," Rev. 13:12.

11. And the beast that was, and is not, even he is the eighth, and is of the seven, and goeth into perdition.

"The beast." When Satan openly poses as the rightful ruler of the New Jerusalem and proposes to lead his deluded followers against it after the thousand years, he becomes the eighth king, GC663, 664; EW293. "Accordingly the beast itself may be identified as Satan," 7BC851.

12. And the ten horns which thou sawest are ten kings, which have received no kingdom as yet; but receive power as kings one hour with the beast.

"The ten horns." Rome's breakup into the divided kingdoms of Europe was to take place after John's day.

"One hour." Prophetic time ended in 1844, EW243, 2SM108. Gr. "a time," suggests no definite length.

13. These have one mind, and shall give their power and strength unto the beast.

"One mind." All nations will have a part, 7BC949. Satan's forces will be united against God's people, with the fourth commandment being the point at issue, 7BC983. The nations will have reached the limit of God's forbearance when a world-wide Sunday law is formulated, 7BC910, and He will make His

presence known when men attempt to enforce the death decree included with this international law, GC635, 636.

14. These shall make war with the Lamb, and the Lamb shall overcome them: for he is Lord of lords, and King of kings: and they that are with him are called, and chosen, and faithful.

"Make war with the Lamb." Christ declared that in the treatment given His followers, "inasmuch," is the treatment given Him, Matt. 25:31–46; so in making war with His people, the forces of evil are making war with Him.

15. And he saith unto me, The waters which thou sawest, where the whore sitteth, are peoples, and multitudes, and nations, and tongues.

16. And the ten horns which thou sawest upon the beast, these shall hate the whore, and shall make her desolate and naked, and shall eat her flesh, and burn her with fire.

"Shall hate the whore." At Jesus' coming the lost will see that they have been deceived by their pastors and teachers, and they turn upon them with fury, using the very weapons they intended to use for the destruction of the Remnant people, GC655, 656; EW290.

17. For God hath put in their hearts to fulfil his will, and to agree, and give their kingdom unto the beast, until the words of God shall be fulfilled.

18. And the woman which thou sawest is that great city, which reigneth over the kings of the earth.

"Great city." Gr. "association."

REVELATION 18

1. And after these things I saw another angel come down from heaven, having great power; and the earth was lightened with his glory.

"Another angel." Joining the third angel, this "loud cry" angel prepares the Remnant for the time of trouble to follow shortly, EW277. It is the last warning message, 7BC985, and produces a genuine revival and reformation, GC464, declaring that Babylon has completely fallen and warns true Christians still within her ranks to leave in order to avoid her punishment, EW278. The work of this angel will be largely brought about by means of the press, 7T140.

"Having great power." The latter rain of the Holy Spirit, an abundant outpouring, prepares the people of God for Jesus' coming, AA55. It is also called "the refreshing" and "the loud cry of the third angel," EW271. But this outpouring cannot come until the Remnant are entirely consecrated as workers for God, ChS253. Because there is but little spirituality among those who believe in Jesus' soon return, God cannot manifest His power more definitely, MM319. But the very same power that the early disciples had is available now for those who work for God, 6T480. The power manifested during the latter rain only angers those opposing, GC607. They are particularly angry at those who accept the warning and attempt to reform, and Satan fans the flames of rage, GC614.

"His glory." This is the message of Jesus' own righteousness, freely offered, sounded throughout the whole earth, bringing to a successful conclusion the third angel's work, 6T19. The whole earth will be flooded with this glory during the latter rain, not just one little corner only, RH, May 10, 1887.

2. And he cried mightily with a strong voice, saying, Babylon the great is fallen, is fallen, and is become the habitation of devils, and the hold of every foul spirit, and a cage of every unclean and hateful bird.

"Babylon." Protestant churches suffered a moral fall in 1844 because of their rejection of the first angel's message, and since then have been falling lower and lower, GC383. The fall is complete when Babylon persecutes those who keep the Sabbath, 7BC980. The entire chapter reveals that the fallen Babylon is the churches that have rejected all the three angels' messages, 2SM68.

3. For all nations have drunk of the wine of the wrath of her fornication, and the kings of the earth have committed fornication with her, and the merchants of the earth are waxed rich through the abundance of her delicacies.

"The wine of the wrath." False doctrines cause this wrath, and when government leaders drink this wine, they become enraged at those refusing to accept such heresies as will cause men to reject the true Sabbath and extol the counterfeit, TM62.

"Her fornication." Actual adultery, fornication, murder, and crime fill the so-called Christian churches, whose pastors are equally guilty, but these things are concealed, 2T449.

4. And I heard another voice from heaven, saying, Come out of her, my people, that ye be not partakers of her sins, and that ye receive not of her plagues.

"My people." The majority of genuine Christians are still in the churches making up Babylon, and this call to them, the last call of mercy to the world, will be heeded, and they will separate themselves from these corrupt organizations, GC390. This call comes during the loud cry, 7BC985. There are many genuine Christians in the Roman Catholic Church, and God will also lead them out of error, CW63, so that when rays of light shine through to them, they will respond, GC565.

5. **For her sins have reached unto heaven, and God hath remembered her iniquities.**

"Her sins have reached unto heaven." Vileness of every stripe is concealed in the nominal churches, but the honest-hearted members will be shown the truth and will come out, 2T449. When the Sabbath is trampled under foot and a counterfeit day of worship is supported by a law of the land, then God will consider that "her sins have reached unto heaven," 7BC977.

6. **Reward her even as she rewarded you, and double unto her double according to her works: in the cup which she hath filled fill to her double.**

7. **How much she hath glorified herself, and lived deliciously, so much torment and sorrow give her: for she saith in her heart, I sit a queen, and am no widow, and shall see no sorrow.**

8. **Therefore shall her plagues come in one day, death, and mourning, and famine; and she shall be utterly burned with fire: for strong is the Lord God who judgeth her.**

"Therefore." God will step in, and to these nominal Protestant churches that have united to glorify Satan, the sentence contained in verse 8 will be pronounced, TM62.

"In one day." Prophetic time having ended in 1844 (EW243, 6BC1052, 2 SM108, 7BC971), this cannot mean the plagues will take a year. In fact, in this very chapter we read, "in one hour," verses 10, 17 and 19.

9. **And the kings of the earth, who have committed fornication and lived deliciously with her, shall bewail her, and lament for her, when they shall see the smoke of her burning.**

10. **Standing afar off for the fear of her torment, saying, Alas, alas, that great city Babylon, that mighty city! for in one hour is thy judgment come.**

11. **And the merchants of the earth shall weep and mourn over her; for no man buyeth their merchandise any more:**

173

"And the merchants." The whole world will suffer poverty and a time of trouble, and even though God's people may suffer hunger, God will be with them to test their faith, Ev240, 241. People of the world will be persuaded by Satan in the guise of a false christ that prosperity cannot return until they rid the earth of those who persist in honoring the Sabbath, GC590. The Remnant will be forced to run from enraged mobs, EW56.

12. The merchandise of gold, and silver, and precious stones, and of pearls, and fine linen, and purple, and silk, and scarlet, and all thyine wood, and all manner vessels of ivory, and all manner vessels of most precious wood, and of brass, and iron, and marble,

13. And cinnamon, and odours, and ointments, and frankincense, and wine, and oil, and fine flour, and wheat, and beasts, and sheep, and horses, and chariots, and slaves, and souls of men.

14. And the fruits that thy soul lusted after are departed from thee, and all things which were dainty and goodly are departed from thee, and thou shalt find them no more at all.

15. The merchants of these things, which were made rich by her, shall stand afar off for the fear of her torment, weeping and wailing,

16. And saying, Alas, alas, that great city, that was clothed in fine linen, and purple, and scarlet, and decked with gold, and precious stones, and pearls!

17. For in one hour so great riches is come to nought. And every shipmaster, and all the company in ships, and sailors, and as many as trade by sea, stood afar off.

18. And cried when they saw the smoke of her burning, saying, What city is like unto this great city!

19. And they cast dust on their heads, and cried, weeping and wailing, saying, Alas, alas, that great city, wherein were made

rich all that had ships in the sea by reason of her costliness! for in one hour is she made desolate.

20. Rejoice over her, thou heaven, and ye holy apostles and prophets; for God hath avenged you on her.

"Ye holy apostles and prophets." Holiness is unreserved yielding to God, living by His Word, doing what He wants us to do, having confidence in Him in discouraging periods, moving along by faith, having confidence in Him without any doubt, and relying on His love, AA51. It is continual harmony with Him, RH, May 16, 1907.

21. And a mighty angel took up a stone like a great millstone, and cast it into the sea, saying, Thus with violence shall that great city Babylon be thrown down, and shall be found no more at all.

"That great city." Gr. "association."

22. And the voice of harpers, and musicians, and of pipers, and trumpeters, shall be heard no more at all in thee; and no craftsman, of whatsoever craft he be, shall be found any more in thee; and the sound of a millstone shall be heard no more at all in thee;

23. And the light of a candle shall shine no more at all in thee; and the voice of the bridegroom and of the bride shall be heard no more at all in thee: for thy merchants were the great men of the earth; for by thy sorceries were all nations deceived.

"Sorceries." "The exercise of supernatural power through the aid of evil spirits," New World Dictionary. Rev. 19:2, "her fornication." "Religion cannot sink lower than when it is somehow raised to a State religion... It becomes then an avowed mistress," Heine, 1822.

24. And in her was found the blood of prophets, and of saints, and of all that were slain upon the earth.

REVELATION 19

1. And after these things I heard a great voice of much people in heaven, saying, Alleluia; Salvation, and glory, and honour, and power, unto the Lord our God:

2. For true and righteous are his judgments: for he hath judged the great whore, which did corrupt the earth with her fornication, and hath avenged the blood of his servants at her hand.

3. And again they said, Alleluia. And her smoke rose up for ever and ever.

4. And the four and twenty elders and the four beasts fell down and worshipped God that sat on the throne, saying, Amen; Alleluia.

5. And a voice came out of the throne, saying, Praise our God, all ye his servants, and ye that fear him, both small and great.

6. And I heard as it were the voice of a great multitude, and as the voice of many waters, and as the voice of mighty thunderings, saying, Alleluia: for the Lord God omnipotent reigneth.

"The voice of a great multitude." After the cleansing fire that purifies the earth, the entire universe unites in making the declaration recorded in this verse, GC673.

7. Let us be glad and rejoice, and give honour to him: for the marriage of the Lamb is come, and his wife hath made herself ready.

"The marriage of the Lamb." While Jesus is in the most holy place, He is married to the New Jerusalem, EW251. God's people are the marriage guests, GC427.

8. And to her was granted that she should be arrayed in fine linen, clean and white: for the fine linen is the righteousness of saints.

"Fine linen." It is the character of Christ, to be received and worn here and now, Ed249, His righteousness, COL310. "The linen is the righteous deeds of God's people," TEV.

9. And he saith unto me, Write, Blessed are they which are called unto the marriage supper of the Lamb. And he saith unto me, These are the true sayings of God.

10. And I fell at his feet to worship him. And he said unto me, See thou do it not: I am thy fellowservant, and of thy brethren that have the testimony of Jesus: worship God: for the testimony of Jesus is the spirit of prophecy.

"The testimony of Jesus is the spirit of prohecy." The testimonies of reproof and of warning are the voice of God, the word of the Lord, 3T258, 362. Satan's final delusion is to try to make of no effect God's messages as given in the writings of Ellen White, since he knows they reveal his wiles and warn against his way of working, 1SM48. While God spoke in Bible times by prophets, he speaks to His people today by the Ellen White writings, and never has he given such careful and detailed information about His will for His people, and He will not accept half-way compliance, 4T148. The Holy Spirit is Author of both the Bible and the Spirit of Prophecy writings, Letter 92, 1900.

11. And I saw heaven opened, and behold a white horse; and he that sat upon him was called Faithful and True, and in righteousness he doth judge and make war.

"Doth judge and make war." "The great battle is not between nation and nation, but between earth and heaven," James White, RH, January 21, 1862.

12. His eyes were as a flame of fire, and on his head were many crowns; and he had a name written, that no man knew, but he himself.

13. And he was clothed with a vesture dipped in blood: and his name is called The Word of God.

14. And the armies which were in heaven followed him upon white horses, clothed in fine linen, white and clean.

15. And out of his mouth goeth a sharp sword, that with it he should smite the nations; and he shall rule them with a rod of iron: and he treadeth the winepress of the fierceness and wrath of Almighty God.

16. And he hath on his vesture and on his thigh a name written, KING OF KINGS, AND LORD OF LORDS.

"King of Kings." Armageddon's battle will be joined when the One described in verse 16 will ride out at the head of Heaven's armies, 6T406. God has a role in the Battle of Armageddon: His armies will come forth, called into action by the agitation of the religious forces, stirred in reaction to the effect of the message of Revelation 18, MS175, 1899. Men bearing weapons of war, driven by demons, hasten to cut down the Remnant, but they are halted by the sudden envelopment of an inky blackness over the earth, followed by God's voice, "It is done," GC635, 636. A small black cloud, "the sign of the Son of man," appears in the east, and Jesus the Conqueror rides forth, GC640, 641. After the delivery of the saints, the wicked cut down one another with the very weapons prepared to kill the saints, EW290, GC656. Especially are they enraged at the unfaithful pastors who have preached lies and made light of what the Bible teaches, 4BC1157.

17. And I saw an angel standing in the sun; and he cried with a loud voice, saying to all the fowls that fly in the midst of heaven, Come and gather yourselves together unto the supper of the great God;

18. That ye may eat the flesh of kings, and the flesh of captains, and the flesh of mighty men, and the flesh of horses, and of them that sit on them, and the flesh of all men, both free and bond, both small and great.

19. And I saw the beast, and the kings of the earth, and their armies, gathered together to make war against him that sat on the horse, and against his army.

"The beast and the kings of the earth and their armies." This is the leopard-like beast of Revelation 13, the papacy, GC445. Under leadership of the papacy the people of the world are united to war against God and persecute His people, 7T182.

20. And the beast was taken, and with him the false prophet that wrought miracles before him, with which he deceived them that had received the mark of the beast, and them that worshipped his image. These both were cast alive into the lake of fire burning with brimstone.

"The false prophet." The beast with lamblike horns, representing Protestantism and/or the United States, Rev. 13:14.

"Worshipped his image." Whatever is served in place of God is thereby worshipped, Matt. 4:10.

21. And the remnant were slain with the sword of him that sat upon the horse, which sword proceeded out of his mouth: and all the fowls were filled with their flesh.

"Slain with the sword," "Our God is a consuming fire," Heb. 12:29. This means that the Holy Spirit destroys sin wherever it is found; those yielding themselves to Him will have sin blotted out, but those attached to sin, cherishing it, will be consumed when sin is destroyed by the glory of Christ at His coming, DA107. "O Israel, thou hast destroyed thyself," Hosea 13:9. God does not destroy anyone; the sinner destroys himself, 5T120, FILB155. That is, the sinner by choosing sin causes a separation between himself and God, thereby cutting himself off from God's blessing, and the resulting ruin and death is a punishment that he has brought upon himself, 6BC1085.

REVELATION 20

1. And I saw an angel come down from heaven, having the key of the bottomless pit and a great chain in his hand.

"The bottomless pit." This describes the world in its battered state after the destruction wrought by the earthquakes and tempests at Jesus' coming, GC658.

"A great chain." Satan is limited to this earth and will not be able to visit other worlds during the thousand years, EW290.

2. And he laid hold on the dragon, that old serpent, which is the Devil, and Satan, and bound him a thousand years,

"A thousand years." When the people of earth are united behind a Sunday law, they declare that the thousand years of peace that they have been looking for has arrived, and in proof of this they point to the wonders and miracles that take place, Letter, January 20, 1884.

3. And cast him into the bottomless pit, and shut him up, and set a seal upon him, that he should deceive the nations no more, till the thousand years should be fulfilled: and after that he must be loosed a little season.

4. And I saw thrones, and they sat upon them, and judgment was given unto them: and I saw the souls of them that were beheaded for the witness of Jesus, and for the word of God, and which had not worshipped the beast, neither his image, neither had received his mark upon their foreheads, or in their hands; and they lived and reigned with Christ a thousand years.

"Judgment was given unto them." Between the first resurrection, when the righteous are raised from the dead, and the second resurrection, when the wicked will be brought to life, a thousand

years transpire, and during the thousand-year period, called the millennium, the righteous in Heaven pass judgment upon the wicked, determining what punishment each shall receive, GC660, since there will be degrees of punishment, Luke 12:47, 48.

"Were beheaded." Many will be martyred before probation closes, Maranatha, page 199, but none after, GC634.

5. But the rest of the dead lived not again until the thousand years were finished. This is the first resurrection.

6. Blessed and holy is he that hath part in the first resurrection: on such the second death hath no power, but they shall be priests of God and of Christ, and shall reign with him a thousand years.

7. And when the thousand years are expired, Satan shall be loosed out of his prison,

"Satan shall be loosed." When the thousand years are over, Christ returns again to the earth and summons the wicked dead to life, and Satan, seeing this vast host, plans to mobilize them to attempt to overthrow the New Jerusalem, which Christ has brought from Heaven, GC662, 663.

8. And shall go out to deceive the nations which are in the four quarters of the earth, Gog and Magog, to gather them together to battle: the number of whom is as the sand of the sea.

9. And they went up on the breadth of the earth, and compassed the camp of the saints about, and the beloved city: and fire came down from God out of heaven, and devoured them.

"Compassed the camp of the saints." Verses 11–13 should be inserted here, for the wicked are judged, and all, including Satan, kneel and acknowledge, before their destruction, that God was right and they were wrong, Isa. 45:23; Rom. 14:11; Phil. 2:9–11; GC669, 670.

10. And the devil that deceived them was cast into the lake of fire and brimstone, where the beast and the false prophet are, and shall be tormented day and night for ever and ever.

"For ever and ever." That is, as long as they live, Exodus 21:6. Some are blotted out in a second while others burn for many days, depending on the number of unforgiven sins each bears, GC673.

11. And I saw a great white throne, and him that sat on it, from whose face the earth and the heaven fled away; and there was found no place for them.

12. And I saw the dead, small and great, stand before God; and the books were opened: and another book was opened, which is the book of life: and the dead were judged out of those things which were written in the books, according to their works.

"The book of life." This book contains the names of those who have yielded themselves to God, 7BC960; those who are counted as God's children, 7BC987; those who have entered God's service, GC480. It also contains the record of the good deeds of the righteous, while the book of death records the wrong acts of the unrighteous, EW52.

"According to their works." Although one is justified by faith, he is judged by works, 4T386. One is not saved by good works, yet he cannot be saved without them, 1SM377. At their judgment the wicked will remember clearly everything they have done without one word or deed escaping their memory, 7BC986. Each one's case will be as carefully scrutinized as if he were the only person on earth, 7BC986.

13. And the sea gave up the dead which were in it; and death and hell delivered up the dead which were in them: and they were judged every man according to their works.

14. And death and hell were cast into the lake of fire. This is the second death.

15. And whosoever was not found written in the book of life was cast into the lake of fire.

"The lake of fire." This fire, consuming the wicked, renovates the earth, GC674.

REVELATION 21

1. And I saw a new heaven and a new earth: for the first heaven and the first earth were passed away; and there was no more sea.

"No more sea." *There will be no oceans in the New Earth, 7BC988.*

2. And I John saw the holy city, new Jerusalem, coming down from God out of heaven, prepared as a bride adorned for her husband.

3. And I heard a great voice out of heaven saying, Behold, the tabernacle of God is with men, and he will dwell with them, and they shall be his people, and God himself shall be with them, and be their God.

"The tabernacle of God is with men." *The places made vacant in Heaven by the rebellion of Satan and his angels will be occupied by God's redeemed people, 7BC949.*

4. And God shall wipe away all tears from their eyes; and there shall be no more death, neither sorrow, nor crying, neither shall there be any more pain: for the former things are passed away.

5. And he that sat upon the throne said, Behold, I make all things new. And he said unto me, Write: for these words are true and faithful.

6. And he said unto me, It is done. I am Alpha and Omega, the beginning and the end. I will give unto him that is athirst of the fountain of the water of life freely.

7. He that overcometh shall inherit all things; and I will be his God, and he shall be my son.

"He that overcometh." It is not possible for the one who indulges appetite to reach the standard of a perfect character, 2T400; but if one conquers appetite, he can overcome any other temptation, HP194; in Christ there is power to control appetite, 9T156.

8. But the fearful, and unbelieving, and the abominable, and murderers, and whoremongers, and sorcerers, and idolaters, and all liars, shall have their part in the lake which burneth with fire an brimstone: which is the second death.

"The fearful and unbelieving." This describes those who are afraid to do right because it might cost something, so their punishment is the second death, 2T630.

"All liars." Any attempt to deceive, a shrug, a wink, or even saying the truth in such a way as to give a different idea from what the words actually say, is a lie, PP309.

9. And there came unto me one of the seven angels which had the seven vials full of the seven last plagues, and talked with me, saying, Come hither, I will shew thee the bride, the Lamb's wife.

"The bride." The marriage between Jesus and the New Jerusalem takes place while He is in the most holy place of the heavenly sanctuary, EW251. God's people are the wedding guests, GC427.

10. And he carried me away in the spirit to a great and high mountain, and shewed me that great city, the holy Jerusalem, descending out of heaven from God,

11. Having the glory of God: and her light was like unto a stone most precious, even like a jasper stone, clear as crystal;

12. And had a wall great and high, and had twelve gates, and at the gates twelve angels, and names written thereon, which are the names of the twelve tribes of the children of Israel:

13. On the east three gates; on the north three gates; on the south three gates; and on the west three gates.

14. And the wall of the city had twelve foundations, and in them the names of the twelve apostles of the Lamb.

15. And he that talked with me had a golden reed to measure the city, and the gates thereof, and the wall thereof.

16. And the city lieth foursquare, and the length is as large as the breadth: and he measured the city with the reed, twelve thousand furlongs. The length and the breadth and the height of it are equal.

"Twelve thousand furlongs." "Fifteen hundred miles long," TEV. The state of Montana, 1,600 miles in circumference approximately, is slightly larger than the New Jerusalem, 1,500.

17. And he measured the wall thereof, an hundred and forty and four cubits, according to the meausre of a man, that is, of the angel.

"An hundred and forty and four cubits." "It was two hundred sixteen feet high," TEV.

18. And the building of the wall of it was of jasper: and the city was pure gold, like unto clear glass.

19. And the foundations of the wall of the city were garnished with all manner of precious stones. The first foundation was jasper; the second, sapphire; the third, a chalcedony; the fourth, an emerald;

"Jasper," green. "Sapphire," blue. "Chalcedony," white. "Emerald," green.

20. The fifth, sardonyx; the sixth, sardius; the seventh, chrysolyte; the eighth, beryl; the ninth, a topaz; the tenth, a chrysoprasus; the eleventh, a jacinth; the twelfth, an amethyst.

"Sardonyx," flesh. "Sardius," red. "Chrysolite," gold. "Beryl," blue. "Topaz," pale green. "Chrysoprasus," pale yellow and greenish. "Jacinth," purple. "Amethyst," violet.

21. And the twelve gates were twelve pearls: every several gate was of one pearl: and the street of the city was pure *gold, as it were transparent glass.*

"The twelve gates." The gates are golden, inlaid with pearls, FILB363.

22. And I saw no temple therein: for the Lord God Almighty and the Lamb are the temple of it.

23. And the city had no need of the sun, neither of the moon, to shine in it: for the glory of God did lighten it, and the Lamb is the light thereof.

24. And the nations of them which are saved shall walk in the light of it: and the kings of the earth do bring their glory and honour into it.

25. And the gates of it shall not be shut at all by day: for there shall be no night there.

"No night there." In the New Jerusalem there is no night, for the glory of God will be brighter than the sun at noon, and in the city no one will require or want sleep, GC676.

26. And they shall bring the glory and honour of the nations into it.

27. And there shall in no wise enter into it any thing that defileth, neither whatsoever worketh abomination, or maketh a lie: but they which are written in the Lamb's book of life.

REVELATION 22

1. And he shewed me a pure river of water of life, clear as crystal, proceeding out of the throne of God and of the Lamb.

2. In the midst of the street of it, and on either side of the river, was there the tree of life, which bare twelve manner of fruits, and yielded her fruit every month: and the leaves of the tree were for the healing of the nations.

"The tree of life." The Garden of Eden, containing the tree of life, was taken to Heaven at the time of the flood, PP62, 8T288.

"Every month." The redeemed will go up to the New Jerusalem from their country homes every Sabbath and every "new moon," Isa. 66:23. Since it would not be in order to gather one's share of the fruit of the tree of life, which has a new crop every month, on the Sabbath, these "new moon" times are perhaps set aside for this purpose.

"The leaves of the tree." The Bible represents the leaves of the tree of life, CT353, as the knowledge given by God, 7BC957. The one receiving Christ's words in his heart understands what eating the leaves of the tree of life means, 7BC957. When God gave men the Word, He gave them a leaf from the tree, 5BC1134, 1135. The leaves had restorative qualities, 3SG35. The Bible, the tree of life, has leaves for healing all who are sin-sick, AA478.

3. And there shall be no more curse: but the throne of God and of the Lamb shall be in it; and his servants shall serve him:

4. And they shall see his face; and his name shall be in their foreheads.

5. And there shall be no night there; and they need no candle, neither light of the sun; for the Lord God giveth them light: and they shall reign for ever and ever.

6. And he said unto me, These sayings are faithful and true: and the Lord God of the holy prophets sent his angel to shew unto his servants the things which must shortly be done.

7. Behold, I come quickly: blessed is he that keepeth the sayings of the prophecy of this book.

"Behold, I come quickly." Suddenly, unexpectedly. The delay is caused by God's pity for His unprepared people, 2T194. Christ would have come before now had His people been ready, Ev644, 645.

8. And I John saw these things, and heard them. And when I had heard and seen, I fell down to worship before the feet of the angel which shewed me these things.

9. Then saith he unto me, See thou do it not: for I am thy fellowservant, and of thy brethren the prophets, and of them which keep the sayings of this book: worship God.

10. And he saith unto me, Seal not the sayings of the prophecy of this book: for the time is at hand.

11. He that is unjust, let him be unjust still: and he which is filthy, let him be filthy still: and he that is righteous, let him be righteous still: and he that is holy, let him be holy still.

"He that is unjust." When this declaration is given, the cases of all will have been judged, CT418; FE363, 364. The door of mercy will be shut when every professed Christian has been examined and human probation will be ended, GC428. God has not revealed the time of probation's close but keeps it a secret, 7BC989, 990. Probation is ended a short time before Christ's return, RH, Nov. 5, 1905. When the angel that does the sealing reports to Jesus that his work is completed, He announces the close of probation, EW279. The time of Jacob's trouble begins at that time, PP201. Records of people's lives are kept up to date daily, 4BC1171, and even hour by hour, 7BC987.

12. And, behold, I come quickly; and my reward is with me, to give every man according as his work shall be.

13. I am Alpha and Omega, the beginning and the end, the first and the last.

14. Blessed are they that do his commandments, that they may have right to the tree of life, and may enter in through the gates into the city.

15. For without are dogs, and sorcerers, and whoremongers, and murderers, and idolators, and whosoever loveth and maketh a lie.

16. I Jesus have sent mine angel to testify unto you these things in the churches. I am the root and the offspring of David, and the bright and morning star.

17. And the Spirit and the bride say, Come. And let him that heareth say, Come. And let him that is athirst come. And whosoever will, let him take the water of life freely.

"The Spirit." The Holy Spirit is a person as much as God, Ev616. He is the most valuable gift that Heaven can give, RH, June 23, 1903.

18. For I testify unto every man that heareth the words of the prophecy of this book, If any man shall add unto these things, God shall add unto him the plagues that are written in this book:

19. And if any man shall take away from the words of the book of this prophecy, God shall take away his part out of the book of life, and out of the holy city, and from the things which are written in this book.

20. He which testifieth these things saith, Surely I come quickly. Amen. Even so, come, Lord Jesus.

"I come quickly." At Jesus' return the physical bodies of the righteous will be changed to be like His, but the character will remain the same; the change in character must take place before His coming, OHC278. When Jesus comes, He is accompanied by

God, and at that time God's people will be far in the majority, AA590.

21. The grace of our Lord Jesus Christ be with you all. Amen.

"The grace of our Lord Jesus Christ." Grace is Christ's power and strength, II Cor. 12:9; His character, COL271; His love, DA389; His Spirit, SC52. "A divine influence, acting in man, to make him pure and morally strong," New World Dictionary.

We'd love to have you download our catalog of
titles we publish at:

www.TEACHServices.com

or write or email us your thoughts,
reactions, or criticism about this
or any other book we publish at:

TEACH Services, Inc.
254 Donovan Road
Brushton, NY 12916

info@TEACHServices.com

or you may call us at:

518/358-3494

Produced in partnership with
LNFBooks.com